YOUNG FAITH

My Story, My Struggles, My Triumph, My Faith

SHALONDA FALCONER
WITH LORIAN TOMPKINS

YOUNG FAITH

SHALONDA FALCONER
WITH LORIAN TOMPKINS

Young Faith

Copyright © 2025 by Shalonda Falconer.

All rights reserved. No part of this book may be reproduced in any form or by any electronic or mechanical means, including information storage and retrieval systems, without permission in writing from the publisher, except by reviewers, who may quote brief passages in a review.

This publication contains the opinions and ideas of its author. It is intended to provide helpful and informative material on the subjects addressed in the publication. The author and publisher specifically disclaim all responsibility for any liability, loss, or risk, personal or otherwise, which is incurred as a consequence, directly or indirectly, of the use and application of any of the contents of this book.

MILTON & HUGO L.L.C.
4407 Park Ave., Suite 5
Union City, NJ 07087, USA

Website: www. miltonandhugo.com
Hotline: 1- 888-778-0033
Email: info@miltonandhugo.com

Ordering Information:
Quantity sales. Special discounts are available on quantity purchases by corporations, associations, and others. For details, contact the publisher at the address above.

Library of Congress Control Number:		2025907848
ISBN-13:	979-8-89285-232-6	[Paperback Edition]
	979-8-89285-643-0	[Hardback Edition]
	979-8-89285-233-3	[Digital Edition]

Rev. date: 07/17/2025

TABLE OF CONTENTS

Preface 13
My Prayer for You 15
Acknowledgements 16
Take These Words with You as You Read 17

Chapter 1:   How It All Began: Momma's Girl 19
Chapter 2:   Me and Momma 26
Chapter 3:   My Young Life Beginning 29
Chapter 4:   Grandma and Grandaddy 40
Chapter 5:   Young Beauty 44
Chapter 6:   A Young Mind Attacked 84
Chapter 7:   Popeye The Sailor Man 96
Chapter 8:   Young and Locked Up 100
Chapter 9:   Bewick 103
Chapter 10: Young and Paid 108
Chapter 11: Young and Taken 113
Chapter 12: I Love Life 159

End-of-Book Poem 162
73 Fun Facts 163
Meet my Co- author 175

OLD PICTURES

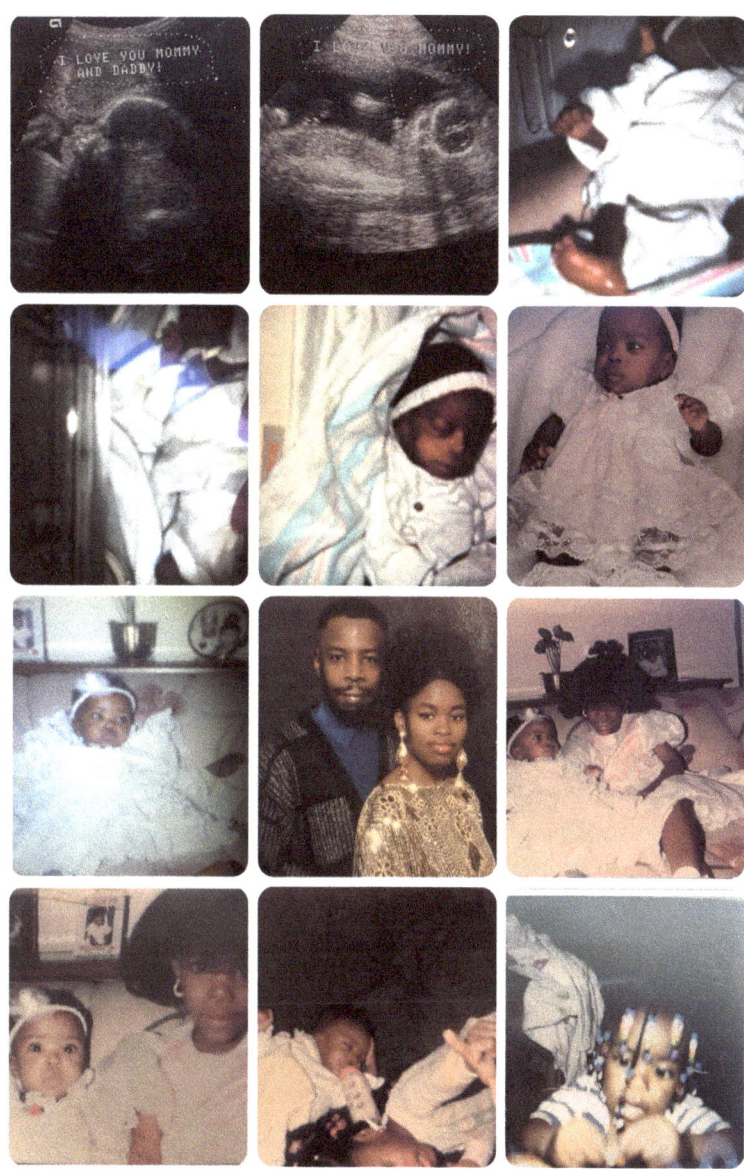

PREFACE

For anyone who has never met me before, I would like to introduce myself: Hello! My name is Shalonda. I am, like many of you, first and foremost a vessel of God, chosen and created for His purpose to do the work needed to expand his kingdom. I am also a daughter, a sister, a fashion designer, a woman once bound by guilt and shame but now set free in Christ—an overcomer, and most importantly, a survivor.

From the time I was two years old, I was well aware of God's presence in my life. Somehow, even at this very young age, something deep inside of me knew that I wanted to please God. Over the years, it became clearer that He had big plans for my life, but I have learned that with every great calling comes opposition in the form of a common enemy that seeks to kill, steal, and destroy. That enemy is The Devil. He hates all that is good and does not like God's people to be happy. He will do whatever he can to stop God's plan for our lives, and it does not matter your age or what family you come from. It doesn't matter how intelligent or talented you are. It doesn't matter how much money you have or what you think you have going for yourself. He will try his best to bring ruin to your life by any means necessary. And he begins this plan very early—as early as possible. Everyone is a target, but those who are called by God and have chosen to follow God are the greatest target of them all.

When I was just sixteen years old, God laid it on my heart to write this book, but at the time, I carried so much guilt and shame that I disqualified myself. I could not see myself the way God saw me because of the struggles I experienced and tried my best to hide. Although I am still on my journey of restoration, I have now reached a place of healing and freedom that enables me to tell my story in full truth—no lies and no fluff. I can speak with boldness and courage because I know that my past does not define me, but instead exists as a testament of God's faithfulness towards me. Through my challenges, He was always with me.

Some of the content of my story includes topics that are often seen as "touchy" in church atmospheres. However, these topics are very real and relevant. They are impacting the lives of so many women, and even men, every single day. So I hope that after reading this book, young women, and young men, will learn the importance of loving themselves and speaking the truth. To anyone who has experienced abuse, please know that even when you feel alone, you are not. Healing takes time and is a process, but it is worth it. God can only heal what is first revealed, so let the revealing take place. If you know in your heart that you were mishandled, do not be silent. Speak out immediately and please never blame yourself for what was done. You deserve love and not abuse. You still have a purpose and can still be all that God created you to be, despite what has happened. Don't let your circumstances define you—instead, let God refine you.

MY PRAYER FOR YOU

Lord, may the individual holding this book hear from you as they read and learn to recognize your voice. Teach them to see things the way you do and see themselves the way you see them. Let them receive spiritual insight, wisdom, and spiritual nourishment. Lord, let these words inspire readers to grow mentally, emotionally, and spiritually. Build up their self-worth and draw them closer to you. I declare and decree that Satan's attacks over their life will not prevail. Let these words help them realize what true love is. May they fulfill your will for their lives, and let them be equipped to do and be everything you want them to be despite what has happened or is happening currently. Break off every bit of fear and timidness and replace it with boldness like a lion's to use their voice. I come against the spirit of suicide, depression, abandonment, rejection, and low self-esteem. I speak life, hope, freedom, and happiness into their life just as Nehemiah 8:10 says, so they can "go and enjoy choice food, sweet drinks" because the joy of the Lord is their strength.

In Jesus's name
Amen.

ACKNOWLEDGEMENTS

I want to thank everyone who has allowed God to lead them to this book. Thank you for taking the time to get to know me and hear my story.

I give glory to God for putting this vision in my heart, giving me the courage to share my story and for introducing Himself to me while I was so young, I also want to thank my family, especially my mom, better known as "Ma mommy," for being such a wonderful example of what The Bible talks about in Proverbs 31.

Thank you to the people who believed in me and helped make this book a reality, including Milton & Hugo, who are the publishers of this book, my amazing sister in Christ and co-author, Lorian Tompkins; my church family who helped ground and mold me spiritually, and every person who has whispered a word of encouragement to me and told me that I was strong, even when I did not believe it. I truly appreciate each and every one of you.

TAKE THESE WORDS WITH YOU AS YOU READ

Young
/yəNG/
adjective

- having lived or existed for only a short time.

    (Oxford Languages)

    Synonyms: *youthful, juvenile, junior, childlike*

    "Don't let anyone look down on you because you are young, but set an example for the believers in speech, in conduct, in love, in faith and in purity.
    (1 Timothy 4:12 New International Version)

Faith
/fāTH/
noun

- complete trust or confidence in someone or something.

(Oxford Languages)

Synonyms: *Trust, belief, confidence, reliance*

"Faith is the substance of things hoped for and the evidence of things not seen… But without faith it is impossible to please him: for he that cometh to God must believe that He is, and that He is a rewarder of them that diligently seek him.
(Hebrews 11:1-6 King James Version)

CHAPTER ONE

HOW IT ALL BEGAN: MOMMA'S GIRL

> For I know the thoughts that I think toward you, saith the Lord, thoughts of peace, and not of evil, to give you an expected end.
> —*Jeremiah 29:11*

> Looking unto Jesus, the author and finisher of our faith, who for the joy that was set before Him endured the cross, despising the shame, and has sat down at the right hand of the throne of God.
> —*Hebrews 12:2*

Once upon a time in the ever so groovy '60s, a young girl named Tracy came into the world on March 5 in the big booming city of Detroit. This little girl did not come from a Christian household. In fact, she lived an average life with a quite imperfect family. Little Tracy had no big dreams aside from one day becoming a mother herself. God was never truly on her mind throughout her childhood, but little did she know, she would be drawn in by His love very soon. He had quite a special life in store for her—one that not only included motherhood, but would also turn her into a mighty woman of God and a revolutionist in her family.

After struggling through the birth of her first child, doctors advised Tracy against having any more children. The complications were so hard on her body that, according to the doctors, it would be smarter for Tracy to throw in the towel and close up her shop early. By this time, she had concluded that having children was simply not her strong suit, as it was for many others, including her own siblings who seemed to conceive and carry easily. In her heart, though, she desired to be a mother of more than just one child. She had the faith to believe that more children were possible, so she didn't give up. However, things weren't so easy and took a while.

After four trying years, God showed Himself faithful and Tracy finally received the news she hoped for in 1992; she found out that she was pregnant with her second child. Hooray! Now Tracy experienced intense difficulties with this baby, even more than she did with her first. No one knew why or what the exact causes were. Her seventh month of pregnancy was very stressful: hemorrhaging came about and she was forced to go to the hospital much sooner than expected.

"There is no heartbeat," The doctors told her. Yikes. It became a situation that could easily have ended up in devastation, But God did the impossible.

On September 28, 1992, a Monday at approximately 6:14 p.m. the baby girl that was expected to arrive later that year in the cozy month of November came twenty eight weeks early at Henry Ford St. John Hospital in Detroit. After the birth, she was immediately rushed into the hospital's neonatal intensive care unit. Tracy could see only a small glimpse of her newly born daughter as the doctors whisked her away the minute she was born. It was a heartbreaking moment of separation. Tracy felt helpless, with nothing more to do than put her faith in God. She needed his peace and comfort during this time of turmoil and unpredictability. Tracy decided to name the baby "Shalonda," without even knowing the name's meaning: *"Sha* and *londa"* combined means "Peaceful Waves."

Scriptures for Encouragement in Childbirth: Genesis 21:6; Amos 9:13–15; Exodus 23:26; Jeremiah 1:5; Psalm 113:9; Psalm 139:14; 1 Corinthians 13:7; 2 Corinthians 4:18

Encouragement, Advice and Reflections

1. Your struggles
2. No longer barren
3. God's date
4. Our plans vs. God's
5. Your children

Maybe you are having struggles in this area too, be it what was mentioned in the story, infertility firsthand or secondhand. Maybe you too long for your child to have a sibling, or maybe you even lost your child, I pray for your comfort!

Scriptures: Psalm 34:18; Psalm 119:50

It's many women in The Bible who struggled with years of barrenness, both Hannah and Sarah did. Sarah had a baby at age ninety years old, literally. Maybe you think that you're too old to have a baby still, but no if God did it for Sarah at her age, He will do it for you, whatever your age. Don't limit yourself. God's blessings have no expiration date. It is not too late to be the mother you dreamed of becoming ten, twenty, or even thirty years ago! God is the ultimate physician—He has the final say! If you are a man reading I am talking to you as well, it's not too late for fatherhood. Male infertility is often less talked about than women's, but I declare life to your reproductive organs. God told Abraham that he'd be a father of many nations and that was so, the same holds true for you!

Scriptures: Genesis 18:11-13; Hebrews 10:35-36; Psalm 103:5; Genesis 17:1-5

Although my expected arrival date was November, God knew exactly what date I'd really be born. Scary. A few years back, God actually gave a shocking revelation to me that I was almost born on September 22, My mom even actually admitted that the doctors at first were going to try to deliver me on that day, but no! God stopped that and made the twenty eighth just for me. God's time is never too early or too late. In His eyes, I wasn't premature I was right on time. God puts us in the right month and on the right day, He even puts us in the right family and in the right generation, all for His unique glory and purpose. Sometimes I think about how things would be if I were born twenty, thirty, forty, fifty or even seventy years sooner, but that wasn't God's divine timing for me.

Scripture: Ecclesiastes 3:11

Maybe you are someone who is facing what they call an "unplanned pregnancy"—say, you're pregnant at a time that may not seem so good for whatever the case, maybe you planned on having a child years later, well God's plans always prevail. God allowed you to conceive for a reason. There is no such thing as an unplanned pregnancy in His eyes. Embrace what you've been blessed with, Don't look at it negatively; ignore any nasty comments. God says that you are qualified. Amen!!! Many people say that you shouldn't have a child if you're not financially stable, but God does what we can't do. Amen! If you are single, no worries. God will fill the other missing part.

Think of this: When Mary discovered that she was pregnant with Jesus, it didn't look exactly ideal, but ultimately, she had to trust what God bestowed on her. Look who she birthed! You don't know who you are going to birth; you may be in for something quite special. Speak and think highly of your child while they are in your womb, children aren't a burden they're a blessing!

Scripture:Psalm 127:3-5

To those patiently and eagerly waiting to become mothers, know this: God sees your children already, and He knows them by name. I myself have gotten countless revelations of mine. Just because you can't see something physically doesn't mean it's not there. It's done in the spirit first. Amen! The spiritual world is real, even more than this natural, earthly world. You are already a mother!

Scriptures:Luke 8:17; Psalm 147:4; 1 Corinthians 2:9; 2 Corinthians 4:18

Part 2

Tracy and her baby girl were inseparable from the time that she could walk. Whether it was traveling to the hair salon to get her signature "Jet-black wet set hairstyle" or playing in her clothes while Tracy decided what outfit she would wear to church next Sunday, they were always together, and everyone around them could feel and see the bond that they shared. They were tighter than glue.

Times were often tough for Tracy and her family, but through it all, she never complained, and God always made a way. For her, having children alone was nothing short of a miracle. Being able to take Shalonda home after what seemed like a hopeless situation was a blessing that she could never forget. Tracy's love for motherhood stemmed from her gratitude toward God, and Shalonda felt this love through her parenting. Tracy started her morning each day with prayer and gospel music playing in the family's home. Shalonda watched, listened, and observed, taking in her mom's practices.

Seeing the way she devoted herself to God inspired her baby girl to do the same. Although she was like an angel to her baby girl, Tracy was not a perfect woman by any means. One of her vices was anger, and she had a very hard time controlling her temper. She refused to tolerate disrespect from anyone, and oddly enough, the name *Tracy* actually means "warlike fighter," which is quite laughable. Shalonda always encouraged her mom to stay calm, but over time, she had to learn on her own how to trust God with that part of herself. No matter what, she knew that God was her everything.

And just as much as He was her everything, He would also require *her* everything.

Scriptures: Ephesians 3:20; Ephesians 4:26; Ephesians 6:12; Deuteronomy 32:35; Exodus 14:14; Ecclesiastes 7:9; Philippians 4:19; Matthew 6:26—27; Psalm 37:25

Encouragement, Advice and Reflections

1. God will fix it.
2. RIP, Mom.
3. Guilt.
4. Mother figures

Maybe you are someone who doesn't have a great relationship with your mom, but God can and will fix it.

Maybe your mom is deceased or wasn't in your life that much. Perhaps you never met your biological mom and instead you had an adoptive mom. Well, whatever the case was, God is everything we need, including a mother.

Scripture: Psalm 27:10

Maybe you're someone reading who feels that you are a bad mom for whatever reason. Maybe you weren't there for your kids like you wanted, and maybe they are even angry at you; but I encourage you to give it to God. He forgives and restores. He softens hearts. Amen!

Maybe you're just an auntie, or simply an older sister who looks out for her younger siblings, know this: your role still holds weight and isn't in vain. Keep doing what you're doing, God sees you! Just like in film, there are so many different roles and some characters have bigger roles than the others, however every role is important; including the background characters.

CHAPTER TWO
ME AND MOMMA

> Behold, children are a gift of the Lord, The
> fruit of the womb is a reward.
> —*Psalm 127:3*

    Whenever my mom would go get her hair done, my sister and I would accompany her. We would be there for hours suffering while she sat to get her jet-black wet set. That was her go-to style, and it became how I identified her as a child. Even if she were a mile away, if I saw just an inch of that curly jet-black hair and burgundy lipstick, I knew instantly that that was my momma. That visual always gave me peace and joy.

    I loved playing in my mom's clothes growing up. I distinctly remember this white T-shirt with colorful gems on the front. This was one of my favorite shirts to play dress-up in. I was devastated one day when I discovered it had gotten thrown away due to an irremovable red stain. How could something so wonderful be tossed in the garbage for something so small? The audacity.

    Other than the heart-wrenching moment, my favorite T-shirt being thrown away, my childhood was wonderful. I remember one day, I told my mom I wanted to be just like her when I grew up. She seemed to genuinely enjoy motherhood. She was attentive, caring, and never complained. My worst nightmares as a kid were the ones of her leaving me or me being separated from her. Some nights I would wake up so relieved that what I experienced was just a dream and momma was still right there next to me.

As someone who did not have an introduction to God growing up, my mom made sure that we watched Christian television programs. She started getting closer to God after I was born. We would all gather in front of the big TV right in the living room, sit on the carpeted floor right in front of the glass coffee table, and listen to the Word of God. At the end, when the speaker said the closing prayer, my mom would put her hands on the TV to agree with them in prayer. I copied her, but instead of using my own hands, for some reason, I thought it necessary to lift my favorite baby doll's hands up in prayer and have her be the one to touch the TV for me.

Every night before bed, my mom, my older sister, and I would all pray The Lord's Prayer. I loved this part of the day. My favorite part of the prayer was the ending stating the power and the glory of God. I envisioned the power to be a cool green color and the glory to be a pretty pink color. I imagined God as a sweet, gentle old man dressed in a gray suit with an everlasting happy face, loving any and every one He saw.

In my early childhood, my mom started out as a proud full-time homemaker. Dinner was always prepared at the right time, and the days were properly organized for my sister and me always ending with a ritualistic bath and bed time. This was how we liked it. But after a while, work became a necessity.

So, my mom picked up a job at the renowned Eastland Mall when I started preschool.

I remember my dad taking my sister and me to the mall to get toys. This was always exciting to me, but the greatest highlight was getting to see my mom.

Together, we would walk through the mall, window-shop, and play with toys that our dad would always cave in and buy for us.

I missed my mom being at home. As a kid, I hated her working, honestly. I mean, why couldn't she just stay home with me all day like she used to? We were just fine with that system in place. I remember telling my mom it felt as though she didn't live in the house anymore. It just didn't feel right.

Although I was not a fan of her being away throughout the day, I eventually adjusted to that decision, as all kids have to. But luckily, she didn't stay away very long and soon returned home. That was a win for me. As I got older, though, she worked more jobs and would often let me tag along. As long as I was with my momma, she could work whatever job she wanted, I didn't care then. Her working didn't stop her from being a mother. She still made time for me, always squeezing into her schedule time to support me in everything that I did, whether it was choir practice or dance lessons and volunteering at my school, until I got of age where I was embarrassed of her volunteering.

Scripture: Matthew 6:9-13.

CHAPTER THREE
MY YOUNG LIFE BEGINNING

Many are called, but few are chosen.
—Matthew 22:14

Part 1

Circa 1994

Barely two years old, Shalonda was still in diapers. Her hair was in thousands of braids, and those braids were covered with thousands of colorful beads. She and her older sister shared a bedroom because the family's home was so small.

In this home, there were only two bedrooms, no upstairs. Everything was all on one floor. There was nice basement, though it was small, but very spacious—nice set-up and perfect for playing and lounging, but basements always scared Shalonda. She never liked being down there alone, her older sister would always be there with her. The two of them would play and ride their bikes down there, her older sister had a cool, sparkly hot pink bike that Shalonda loved and wanted to ride, but she was too small, of course. Eventually, Shalonda got a red tricycle that she rode down there.

Shalonda admired her older sister and knew that she was very smart, as she taught her a lot of things. Shalonda wanted to go to school with her, but due to their four-year age gap, that was impossible. Shalonda became curious about school, seeing her go every morning. She missed her sister while she was gone and loved seeing her come home with her school assignments. This intrigued her ever so much.

Shalonda and her sister loved going to get snacks around the corner. Afterwards, they would chill in the living room in front of the TV and watch their favorite TV shows, which consisted of *Rugrats, Doug, "Aaaah!" Real Monsters, Clarissa Explains It All,* and many more.

One thing was for sure: God was with Shalonda during those early years of her life. She used her faith for pretty much anything, literally!

I can remember very vividly my oldest sister and I having a white bed covered with rainbow-bright bedding, It was so high off the floor that I could barely climb into it each night. It didn't help that I was so small for my age. I could get in that bed only if someone lifted me; however, I was always determined to be able to climb into the bed by myself, as I was very tenacious.

In my mind, I wasn't small at all, and there wasn't anything that I couldn't do. I was not a baby. I remember I even hated when people would refer to me as such. I desired to be seen as a big kid like my older sister.

One thing that fascinated me at this young age was seeing my shadow, because it made me look so much bigger. This greatly intrigued me. As believers, we may be small in the physical realm, but in The Spirit, we are giants, and we can climb no matter how high. Amen! However, the times when we do struggle, God will lift us up to the top. Amen! Our shadow is The Holy Spirit, who's huge. He is in our small bodies making us much bigger.

Scriptures:Psalm 91:1; 1 John 4:4; Romans 8:37

Along with my tenacity also came hunger—a hunger for God. I was a very curious child, always wondering about the things of God. "Where did God come from," I would ask my mom. "Who created Him?" "Well," my mom would say, "God was just always here." Her simple answers to my big, but small questions made me appreciate God even more. I loved hearing my mom confirm that what I discovered in my *Little Precious Moments Kids' Bible* was actually true. God was always here, yes.

He created everything, yes. No one made Him, but He, in fact, made everything, yes. And yes, He loved all of His little children. I remember one thing that stood out to me the most, and that was "You can't hide from God." No matter what, God can see you. I remember in my little Precious Moments Bible there was a picture where the little child was trying to hide under his blankets on his bed, but he knew God could still see him wow. That always stayed in my mind.

Scriptures:Matthew 5:6; Hebrews 4:13—15

Another scripture that had stood out to me and that I learned to recite by heart was Psalm 23. I remember having vivid images in my mind of what the things talked about in that passage looked like. This scripture contributed to my trust in God even more.

I always had the peace of God, despite all that was going on in my family; the problems that were happening just flew over my head. The Devil could not take my joy; I always trusted and knew that God was going to make a way always, and He did. Amen! I remember my mom said that God could do everything but fail, and this I soon began to witness.

At this early stage of my life, I experienced The Devil trying to put a physical ailment on me. I had an issue with my head that would need some quick medical intervention; however, God instantly provided me relief. I got prayer at church, and the issue immediately resolved and never came back. Amen!

Part 2

I remember I couldn't help but wonder about the people who choose to follow The Devil instead of God. My mom made it very clear to me that The Devil hated everyone—even those who chose to follow him. She explained that nothing good would come to them and they were just being used unknowingly, but The Devil was glad that he had deceived them. I remember us one night reading The Bible and having a conversation about Heaven and Hell. My mom asked me where I wanted to go. I was unsure, but she explained and made it very clear to me that if I went to Hell, I'd be completely suffering with no way out; but if I went to Heaven, I'd never have any problems ever again. Although I was so young, this conversation resonated deeply with me. This made me take the things of God more seriously.

Scripture: Proverbs 22:6

Although I had such a passionate zeal for God and was in church, It was a few years down the line that I realized that there was one important thing missing from my life. I realized that I wasn't truly saved; I wasn't a true believer because I had not yet personally accepted Jesus into my heart with open confession. I just was in church and read The Bible and knew about God and the things of God, but I recognized that wasn't enough. I was ten years old when I realized this, and I knew it was an important decision I had to make immediately. I remember the day so vividly. It was winter-time, and my mom had given me a cute press-and-curl hairstyle, and I wore a red-and-black checkered dress. Now I gotta be honest: at the end of service, when the altar call came for salvation, I grew doubtful and hesitated in going up. I vividly remember hearing that going to Hell actually wouldn't be that bad and that I would be able to handle being there. "Yikes" I immediately knew that was The Devil and I refused to obey him. I immediately stepped out my seat and made my way to the altar, and tears of joy came down my face. I felt relief knowing that I had made the best decision for my life: Heaven was now my home. I felt "refreshed." I was so excited the whole rest of the day after church had ended.

Now for many people, they grew up in church. They just go to church because it's simply what they're used to and they believe that's all they have to do. Many people go to church just out of tradition—because it was something taught by their parents and grandparents, but church attendance itself, Bible reading, baptism, praying, or simply knowledge of God alone does not equate to salvation. Salvation is a heart matter—it's a personal decision and requires a personal relationship, commitment.

If you are reading my book and you attend church, know about God, pray, read your Bible, that's good, but I must ask you: Are you truly saved? This is a very important question to know the answer to, and it's important to make a decision in this area as soon as possible.

Don't delay, none of us knows how long we have on this earth. God does give us time, but time will eventually run out. I remember at a church that I attended there were some young guys who said they would eventually get saved.

Literally they'd always say "eventually." However, one day, they didn't make it to church, and they had gotten into a car accident. I'm not sure if they died in the accident—and no them getting into an accident wasn't God punishing them for not accepting Him, but it's a reality on why it's important to obey God quickly when He tells you to do something because you don't know what may come your way. When you're not a believer, you don't have the full benefits of being a child of God which includes His protection, provision, etc.

God will still look out for you, but it's way easier for The Devil to attack you. He will still attack you as a believer, but you're double-protected if you're a believer; We have God protecting us, The Holy Spirit in us guiding us, and our assigned angels.

I think about if I hadn't made the decision at ten years old, who knows what would've happened to me. All glory to God for leading me to Him early on! I don't take it for granted at all!

Part 3

Although I had made the big decision and was now a true believer, I struggled greatly with doubting my salvation; literally, I constantly feared losing it. I thought that I would need to repeat going to the altar again. I feared ending up in Hell by any small error. I remember at a church that I attended, it was even said that any little thing could result in going to Hell. "Yikes." That produced more fear in me. I believed that salvation was a works righteousness thing, meaning I believed I could earn my salvation only by behaving well. In reality, many believers feel and think this way. It is the lie of The Devil. He will do any and everything to deter us from the path God has for us. Doubt and lies are his greatest tools. This is why it's so important to know the truth of God's Word. The

Bible says to put on the whole armor of God. It also says that we are not ignorant of Satan's devices.

Don't be led by how you feel; instead, be led by what you know. Scripture says that you shall know the truth, and the truth shall set you free. Your new life is now beginning. You are a young believer, but it's just the beginning of all that God has in store for you! Stay tuned, and you will grow more and more.

Surround yourself with like-minded people too. Don't do this journey alone.

Scriptures: Proverbs 13:20; Proverbs 27:17;1 Thessalonians 5:11; Ecclesiastes 4:9– 12; Philippians 2:1— 8; 1 Corinthians 15:33; 2 Corinthians 6:14

Encouragement, Advice and Reflections

1. Accept Jesus
2. Spreading the gospel
3. Never alone
4. Salvation truths
5. Salvation confirmation
6. Using your faith in small ways
7. Tired
8. Have some fun

If you're not a believer but desire to become one please recite this prayer, you can do it alone or with others, say, supportive family and friends who are saved, but it's okay to do it alone because ultimately, it's a personal decision, here it is:

Dear Heavenly Father,

I'm sorry for the wrong things I've done. Please forgive me. I believe that you sent your Son Jesus to die on a cross for my sins, and I believe that He rose from the dead on the third day by the power of The Holy Spirit, and because of this, I will enter heaven when I die. Jesus, come into my heart and be my Lord and Savior. Save me from sin. I willingly give you my life. Now, Father, help me do your will. Thank you again for saving me! In Jesus's name I pray. Amen.

If you've prayed this prayer and you truly believe in your heart, the key is believing—belief is powerful; you can say something out of your mouth and still not believe it, I can assure you that if you truly believe after praying this prayer, then you are, indeed, truly saved, and your best life is ahead of you. Continue to believe all of God's promises. Let's celebrate! Allow The Holy Spirit to lead your life, and let Him lead you to the church home He has for you.

Scriptures: John 3:16—18; 1 john 1:9; Romans 6:23; Romans 10:9— 13; Isaiah 1:18; 1 Peter 2:9; 2 Peter 3:8— 10; 2 Corinthians 5:17; Luke 15:7; Matthew 5:13—16; Matthew 6:24; Acts 16:30—33

After I got saved, my sisters, brothers, and dad all followed suit.

Scriptures: Isaiah 11:6; Joshua 24:15

When I was in middle school, God led me to buy a friend of mine a Bible. I remember very vividly buying it at this Christian bookstore called the "Tree of Life." This friend greatly appreciated this gift and even brought it and read it at school.

In high school, I had invited two friends to church, and they went up to the altar for salvation.

At one of my old churches, I was a part of the team that would go out and witness to non-believers. The team was called the SWAT team. I enjoyed it! As believers, we can't save people however, we can plant the seed. Amen!

Scriptures: Mark 16:15; Isaiah 52:7

You may feel alone and misunderstood on this new journey, but rest assured that you are not alone. The Bible says that God will never leave us or forsake us. Amen! Not everyone will understand your journey, and that's okay. You may lose some people, and that's okay! The Bible says we must take up our own cross to follow Jesus. Once we are believers, it's not just about ourselves anymore—it's about Him. We must let go of our own ways, plans, and desires and follow the ways, plans, and desires of God.

Scriptures: Matthew 6:33; Luke 22:42; John 6:38

Salvation is not works righteousness, thankfully. It's not about being perfect or doing everything right! God knows we can't do anything on our own strength, and that's not what He expects or wants us to do. He sent His son Jesus Christ to die for us so that Jesus Himself could be our salvation! That's why we must accept Jesus into our hearts, and we must believe in Him and not in our own selves. When we become believers, after believing and accepting Jesus into our hearts, that's when The Holy Spirit comes to live inside of us, and He empowers and equips us to live out what Jesus provided for us which is salvation, healing, love, etc. We are more than conquerors through Jesus. Our salvation is fully in Him. Please cut yourself some slack. God meets us where we're at. He is not the authoritarian type of parent that you may have had growing up. He is a loving parent who doesn't give up on us, and He doesn't put unrealistic expectations on us, because He knows that we can fall, which is why He sent Jesus to die for us. The Bible is clear that He doesn't want anybody to perish!

Although I have had many doubts in this area of my life, God always confirmed to me that I really am saved and belong to Him and have eternal life. He has confirmed this for me through dreams, scriptures, songs, and at times, even random words in the dictionary. One time I was struggling to believe that I was really saved and would enter heaven, but He had me look up the word *invincible* in the dictionary. Now, some synonyms of *invincible* are *indestructible*, *safe*, *secure*, and *unyielding*. God will always confirm things when we have doubts and that's in every area. All His promises hold true. Amen!

When I was in the eighth grade, every single morning that I got dressed, I would always get a small piece of paper, and I would write "Jesus" on it. Then I would stuff it in my sock. I did this as a way to use my faith to have a good, peaceful, and safe day at school. I believe this worked for me as my school days were peaceful and safe for the most part, however, not saying that you have to do that. It's whatever you are led to do personally. God moves with us where our faith is at and how we choose to use our faith, as long as it lines up with His will. We have the power to make our day. Amen!

Let's be honest if you grew up in church, have you ever found it boring or gotten tired and felt like, *"Yeah, I've heard and seen this all before——enough.* Maybe you even, at one point, contemplated leaving the church. Well, if you felt this way, it's not a sin, as we are still human. Sometimes church can seem repetitive; however, don't get the church building itself and the people and things inside confused with God. Even the church can come with its pitfalls, but God doesn't come with any flaws, thankfully, and He certainly doesn't desire to bore us. Some churches have many rules, but God is not a set of rules. Don't judge Him based on an experience at church. Judge Him by getting to know Him personally. Think about it, if we judge another person by a experience we have with them at school or at work or just on the street. A experience is not as personal as a relationship. Many ask, Do you have to go to church to be saved? Well, truthfully, no you don't, however, church attendance does have benefits.

Can you do activities that are non-church? Say, movies, mall, concert, or even a party! The answer, yes, with movies and music ultimately, know the difference between fantasy and reality. These two things often portray fictional events for the most part, which I believe is not harmful; however, if you're a person who is bothered by gory and scary things, then perhaps you shouldn't watch and listen. Now, if a song is blatantly cursing God, or if it's a song that's dragging you down, then yeah, change your playlist! Listen to music that gives you joy and lifts you up!

Can music and movies make you sin? Well, in my opinion, I'll say no because the decision to sin is our very own choice. Temptation is always going to be around in every form, but we are in control of our own actions. If you sin, it's not because of a movie that you watched or a song that you listened to. It was a desire in you that you chose to act on willingly. Of course, bad desires come from The Devil—he is the one who tries to get us to sin ultimately, but we have authority over him, remember that.

Scriptures: James 1:14; Galatians 5:16—26; Ephesians 4:27—30

CHAPTER FOUR
GRANDMA AND GRANDADDY

I was very close to my paternal grandparents, although my desire to follow God was always there, they also played a role in me following God. If you've ever seen the '70s sitcom *Good Times*, I can attest that my grandparents were just like *Florida and James Evans*.

My grandma was a loving, prayerful woman just like Florida, She loved her children and did the best she could, and she was also a homemaker like Florida was in the early seasons of the sitcom, literally. My grandma never ever worked; she just stayed home with the children and tended to the house. My granddaddy was just like James Evans—very hardworking and no-nonsense with the children, but he still loved his family and did the absolute best he could with the little he had like James Evans, he wasn't rich or had a high-paying job, and he wasn't highly educated like James Evans either, but they both did their best and relied on God.

Neither of my grandparents grew up in church or came from Christian families themselves. My grandmother walked to church by herself at ten years old every Sunday. My grandfather didn't follow God until years later into his adulthood. My grandparents had loads of children and grandchildren. My sisters and I were way at the very end of all their grandkids. My grandfather was crazy about me; his nickname for me was "Baby Boo," and our birthdays were in the same month, ten days apart, his birthday was September 18.

I remember my grandparents ate from the company Meals on Wheels. As a child, I thought that Grandma and Grandaddy were my grandparents' actual real names. Once I found out their actual names, I was shocked and fascinated. My grandmother, I remember, loved the store Farmer Jack, which no longer exists. She had gotten lost in there quite a few times.

Early in my childhood, my older sister and I would often go to my grandparents's house, however, I must admit that neither me nor my sister really liked the house that they lived in, and we would play outside instead. We thought their house was haunted after all, it was really, really old.

Outside was super cool, as they had a garden in the backyard that we loved. My grandparents always made us feel loved every time we went over to their house.

They supported us in everything that we did, including our church activities.

For a while, we attended their church. I did enjoy going to this church; I have very vivid memories of Sundays there, as well as vacation Bible school. My grandfather was a deacon at this church.

Now my grandmother eventually ended up falling ill and was put in a nursing home. The whole family went up there to visit her as often as possible, For me, I had peace although she was dying.

I remember thinking I was going to be able to see her spirit go up to Heaven. Going to Heaven always fascinated me.

My grandma ended up actually dying in her birth month, May; she died right around Mother's Day. She didn't even get to meet my little sister, who was the very last grandchild, born the month prior. I remember how much she had looked forward to meeting her. Sigh.

My grandfather lived for a few short years after her, but he began to get dementia and had mini strokes from time to time. I remember he was at the house one day and I put an orange sweater on my head, and he thought it was actually my hair, literally, He died in January 2003. I remember getting the news when I got home from school. I was shocked. I remember after he died, I just had a bit of a difficult time sleeping. I would see vivid images of him in the house in my mind. It felt so odd, him being gone. I would mainly have vivid memories of what he wore, his jacket and pants. I was bummed out from his death because he was the only grandfather I was close to, so now I was basically without a grandfather. I remember that for his funeral, I wrote a lovely poem, but oddly enough, I didn't cry at his funeral, or even at my grandmother's funeral.

Scriptures: Isaiah 46:4–5; Proverbs 16:31, 17:6; Psalms 92:14; Luke 1:50

Encouragement, Advice, and Reflections

1. Loss
2. Life after for believers
3. Mourning
4. Heaven the truth
5. Comfort in unique ways

You may have physically lost those close to you, whether it was your grandparents, your actual parents, or a close friend. But I can attest to you that if they were believers, they are in Heaven living it up, though you don't see them anymore. We have the promise of eternal life, not only for ourselves, but our saved family and friends as well. Now, it is okay to cry and to have moments where we may feel down, but we don't have to stay down! When we mourn, which it's truly okay to do, our comforter is The Holy Spirit. Amen!

Scriptures: Matthew 5:4; Psalm 30:5

Think about this: When Jesus died on the cross many people were down about it, but on that third day He rose again Amen! He conquered death, Hell and the grave!

Scriptures: Luke 23:43; 1 Thessalonians 4:13—18; 2 Corinthians 5:8; Philippians 3:20—21; Revelations 21:4; Isaiah 26:19

As a child, I always envisioned Heaven as a fun, pretty place in the sky, particularly located on top of the clouds and filled with endless happiness. Now to an extent, this is true, however, Heaven is more than just cuteness, fun, clouds, and even happiness. It's a place of fellowship with God, There is unending joy, yes. It's a place for glorifying God with other believers, It's a spiritual place, It's unseen in the natural world. When I was younger, I thought that I could build a long tower to reach up to Heaven. But no, we will see Heaven only spiritually, The Bible says that flesh and blood can't enter Heaven. Why? Because if we went to Heaven in our flesh, we wouldn't be able to truly understand it, or probably even fully appreciate it. Once we truly get to Heaven, we won't be in earthly bodies—meaning that we won't be thinking in an earth1y mindset. We will view everything the way God does.

I never dreamed about either of my grandparents after they were dead, but what's funny is that sometimes I'd feel their presence in the house, and even smell their scents. My grandmother loved the candy orange slices, and at times that's exactly what I would smell. God has ways of giving us comfort when we lose our loved ones. I have a tattoo on my chest in remembrance that says "Grandaddy 2003."

CHAPTER FIVE
YOUNG BEAUTY

Part 1: Airless

It's a beautiful fall morning—the kind of day where the leaves have just begun to change as a reminder that the warm summer months have packed their bags and are preparing to leave. The air is wet from rain, with the cool breeze that lingers after the sun comes out. In the distance, I can hear laughter, screams, footsteps hitting the pavement, and that squeaking sound the swing sets make every time a kid goes up and comes back down. I see the joy on faces that are so relieved to be out of that boring classroom that they make sure to soak in every moment that outdoor recess will bring them. But instead of basking in that joy myself, I am sitting and watching from the sidelines, trying to catch my breath. Today, like most days, I could play for only a few minutes before the air that I longed for just minutes earlier becomes an enemy attempting to suffocate me. With my inhaler clenched tightly in my fist so no one can see it, I stand on the sidelines in shame, wondering why my body wouldn't allow me to play like other kids.

When I was a child asthma was an aspect of myself that made me begin to dislike who I was. From the time that I was diagnosed at the age of four years old, I spent many days feeling excluded from activities that involved a lot of movement. Although I was not the only kid on the planet with asthma, there was something about it that made me feel like an outcast. To me, asthma was a flaw that proved that I was less than the other kids.

I felt terribly ashamed whenever I needed to use my inhaler. To erase some of the shame, I tried my best to hide it.

When others would notice my struggles with breathing and ask if I had asthma, I would always deny it. And during moments where I needed to take my other many medications, I tried to do it in places where no one could see me.

No one had to tell me that I was different from other kids because I knew it. And in my mind, this difference only highlighted the fact that I was broken in ways that no one could fix. At this young and tender age, I had already witnessed one of the many ways The Devil would look to destroy my confidence from the inside out.

Before this devastating diagnosis, my health seemed pretty okay to me. I would catch colds every now and then, but they were never bad enough to require hospitalization or anything close. But one day, while at my grandparents' house, I had randomly gotten so sick to the point where I couldn't move. I remember just lying there, unable to speak while my body screamed in pain. It was so excruciating that words couldn't come out of my mouth. The adults in the room began to gather, growing more and more concerned and wondering what to do. My aunt finally called my mom while she was at work and told her what was going on with me.

My mom left work and rushed over to get me. When we arrived at the hospital, I was immediately diagnosed with asthma. I will never forget the way my heart dropped and the shame that came over me when I heard them say that word. I didn't want anyone in the family to know I had this burdensome disease, but it began to take over my life in a way that was impossible for others around me to ignore.

My attacks were extreme, to the point where I was hospitalized every time each one occurred. As it became a habit, I knew during every one that my next stop would be the hospital. What we expected to be a few hours there always turned into longer than just a short couple hours, or even a few days. It always turned into weeks, and in the worst cases, weeks would turn into nearly a full month.

I absolutely hated that me and my broken body were such a bother to my family more specifically—my mom. She would often wake up to the sound of her daughter's endless wheezing, struggling to catch her next breath. We would have to go to the hospital sometimes at 2:00 or 3:00 a.m. just to deal with my sudden attacks. There were times when I would just try to handle things on my own. I even remember one time trying a home remedy to cure my impending asthma attack, but of course, it did me no good.

It got to the point where I was embarrassed to even tell my mom when I wasn't feeling well. Sensing my shame, she would try to reassure me that it was okay and that I was not making her life harder. She was my mom, and she was okay with taking care of me. But, this never stopped me from feeling the way I felt.

Asthma played no games with me. I always needed a wheelchair when I got to the hospital because the attacks would beat me down and weaken my body so much. My chest would often feel as though it were on fire, which made it impossible to speak, eat, and drink. The intense pain that plagued every inch of my body made it difficult for me to even get up to use the bathroom. Yikes. My mom would just bring me my food on a tray as I lay there. The Devil attacked my mind so much during this time, specifically in the area of self-value. He convinced me that I was so abnormal that I wasn't worthy of love. He made me believe that my parents secretly wished that they had a different child—a better child, one that was healthy and without issues like me. Sigh.

Asthma greatly affected my school attendance. I would miss loads of school, which I didn't want to do. Most of my teachers knew about my struggle, and they were supportive. I remember one teacher wrote some encouraging words to me on my report card. Many times I'd press on to go to school, but I'd have to leave early. Sigh. One time my mom gave me a breathing treatment right while I was at school, although she didn't do it in my classroom and did it privately away from everyone I was completely mortified. In high school, I'll never forget at my tenth grade homecoming dance, I had got sick and had to go to the hospital immediately afterward.

Scriptures: Isaiah 53:5; James 5:14; Mark 5:34; 2 Corinthians 5:7; Matthew 9:18-26; Matthew 15:28; John; 2:11; Psalm 77:14; Jeremiah 32:27; Luke 1:37; Hebrews 2:4

Encouragement, Advice, and Reflections

1. The power of the voice
2. Jesus's lungs
3. High value
4. Words
5. God recognizes your voice
6. Birthday Faith
7. Laugher is good medicine
8. Grateful

I remember early in my childhood, I had a dream that my voice was completely gone. No matter how hard I tried, when I opened my mouth, nothing would come out. I woke up frantically checking my voice to make sure that my vocal chords were still intact. When I discovered that they were, I was so relieved.

Obviously, the lungs are necessary for one to be able to use their voice, for one to breathe. Just think for a minute about Jesus on that cross. He was out of breath; His voice was gone, literally. He took on every single lung disease! Yikes.

Even if you don't have any issues with your lungs breathing in harmful chemicals can be extremely dangerous and deadly for anyone. Jesus breathed in the sins of the world literally. All of that harm He took in but for us so we didn't have to.

The areas that The Devil attacks us in the most are often the areas that hold the most power and value. At one church that I attended the pastor always said that thieves don't break into empty houses. This statement is so true, A thief will only go into a house that has lots of valuables inside it!

Scripture: Proverbs 6:31

Words have so much power. What we say and believe affects our lives. Every time someone—even doctors—asked me if I had asthma, I would always say "No." Although the root of this was shame, there was still a level of faith in operation. I had always known that the issues happening in my body weren't supposed to be there, nor did I want them there. That belief subconsciously manifested in how I spoke about them to others and myself. I believe that contributed to my healing over time. At the same church I mentioned above, the pastor would also say that loose lips sink ships, which meant our words can either lift us up or cause us to drown. Amen!

Scripture: Hebrews 10:35—37

What we say to God and what we say to ourselves, internally and externally, is never in vain. Whether it's positive or negative, it has the power to become, as The Bible calls it, the "fruit" of our life. Our outcomes are impacted by our words.

Be intentional in what you say and what you believe! Amen.

Scriptures: Mark 11:23; Proverbs 13:2; Luke 19:40; Romans 15:6–7; Psalm 22:3; Psalm 30:12; Psalm 34; Psalm 150:6; Isaiah 49:13

I remember one night reading a book about the miracles Jesus performed while on the earth, I wasn't feeling 100 percent, yet my mind was made up. I didn't want to get sick, so before drifting off to sleep, I had prayed and asked God for me to be fully healed in the morning. I woke up, and this was indeed fully so. God heard my voice and did exactly what I asked for. Amen!

Although there are many voices coming at God at once, He distinctly recognizes your voice. He doesn't get your voice mixed up with someone else's even if you whisper, He can hear your voice loud and clear.

Scriptures: 1 Peter 3:12; Ephesians 3:20; John 16:24

I remember my ninth birthday like it was yesterday, what remember the most and what made me the happiest was God healing me directly on my day. Amen! I thought the day would be ruined, but no, it was the absolute best day ever! Ironically, on that day I wore the color green, which biblically represents rest, renewal, and immortality. God is so strategic.

I remember when I'd be in the hospital, my mom would crack jokes to make me feel better, and it worked. I was just happy that I could get something out of my mouth. The more that I laughed was just evidence of God's healing upon me. Amen!

Scripture: Job 8:21

I must forever be grateful because I realize that there are many individuals who didn't make it through asthma. There are millions of people who died due to fatal asthma attacks. I realize that could've been me. Unfortunately, many mothers took their child to the hospital during the same time that my mom took me, and unfortunately, those kids didn't get any better, and the doctors had to deliver the bad news. Imagine if my mom hadn't been able to bring me back home. Yikes. Asthma can be mild or severe; my asthma was severe. I recognize that God definitely is real, and He definitely kept me. Him keeping me is a clear sign that He had a plan for my life that He refused to let be stopped. Amen!

To those reading who have lost a child or loved one from a fatal asthma attack, my sincere condolences to you! To those like myself who survived severe asthma, please don't take things for granted. Always remain grateful. You are here for a reason, so show up and show out! If you are reading my book and struggling with a potentially fatal asthma attack, I speak life to your lungs. You will live; you will not die. Breathe out God's goodness and his promises!

Scripture: Isaiah 54:17

References
- 5 Tips to Prevent Asthma Flare-Ups This Fall by the editorial Each Breath October 13, 2022
- Asthma + Lung UK
- Life with a lung condition

Part 2: Another Diagnosis

After so many years of fighting with my health, I was finally starting to get a grip on it around age eleven. Although I was still battling with my self-image, I was so proud of my progress. Now that I was headed into the glorious preteen era, I was ready to start over. This would be my time to feel more like a normal kid. Shalonda could finally do Shalonda. Yippee.

I was ever so eager to buy new clothes and show off my cute, developing figure. I was no longer a little girl. I was on the road to becoming a woman, and I was so excited for the adventure that it would bring. But, little did I know that adventure would quickly end before it could even truly begin.

In 2003, something extremely unexpected happened. I was diagnosed with scoliosis. *Oh no!* I thought. Just like my asthma diagnosis, I was shocked, embarrassed, numb, and couldn't believe it. Here I was, literally reliving the shame all over again. Although I was older this time around and a bit more mature, one thing that hadn't changed since childhood was my dislike for attention.

After the diagnosis, people at church, school, and even family would approach me to check on how I was feeling and ask if I was okay. I knew they meant well, but it only made me feel even more pitiful. Sighs.

After all that asthma put me through, the last thing I wanted was for another illness to become a part of my identity. I did not want to be "the girl with scoliosis," Especially when high school was right around the corner. It was hard enough getting over asthma—now this? I immediately got put in a back brace after my initial diagnosis. And boy, oh boy, was this my worst preteen nightmare.

Wearing that brace was so awkward and uncomfortable. It was ruining my new cute figure. *How can I be fashionable now?* I thought. How would I wear a tube top or a tank top in the summertime? How would I rock my midriffs? How would I have fun with new friends? How would I play or swim or do cartwheels in the grass? This diagnosis had already begun to rob me of all the joy I was looking forward to experiencing as a preteen. Most importantly, it began to rob me of what little self-esteem I had left.

For quite a while, my soul longed for a miraculous healing. I would watch charismatic preachers on television help people instantly receive healing. One of these men even held a conference in Michigan where we lived. My mom, my sisters, and I all went. I hoped with all my heart that this would be my time at this event. Yet nothing happened. I left out the exact same. Sighs. I became more and more discouraged as time passed, and even became bitterly rebellious against the doctors' orders. I had a time limit on how long I was supposed to wear my brace throughout the day, but I started refusing to wear it. I would even sneak away and take it off at school.

While my wildest dream was that this would one day be healed, the scoliosis just got worse and worse. Every doctor's visit ended with a disappointing report.

My spine had curved in such an unnatural way that it pretty much formed into the shape of an S. It was no secret that surgery would more than likely be a necessary option. The doctors suggested that I stop wearing the brace and told my family to consider surgery as soon as possible. I was not a fan of this. *Surgery is for old people*, I thought. *I'm too young for that. And what if the surgery goes wrong?* Yikes. In my heart, I simply wanted God to be the one to fix me, not surgery. I longed for a miracle, but it never came. So, I eventually had to consider this other option just like everyone else.

Encouragement, Advice, and Reflections

1. Waiting for healing
2. Decisions
3. God first
4. No limits on God

I had desperately wanted to be healed, but I couldn't make it happen in my own way. One time my desperation made me consider buying some so-called healing water that I had seen on a Christian network, but thankfully, I didn't have peace with that.

As you are waiting and praying for a breakthrough in an area, never act out of desperation, As this can lead to poor decision-making that is based on your *own* understanding. Instead, remain obedient to God and have trust in Him, no matter how it looks.

Scriptures:1 Samuel 15:22; Proverbs 3:5- 7; Psalm 118:17—18

We all have to make difficult decisions at times. When we are uncertain or fearful, it's not easy. But, you have to know that God is with you always. The Holy Spirit will lead and guide you through your difficult decisions if you allow Him to. We never have to do things alone. While you're waiting for your healing, don't create your own expectations of how it will come. It may even come through the difficult decision you're hesitant to make.

If you keep God at the center, He will send you the confirmation that you need to go forward with the best plans for your life. The route to your answered prayer may not look exactly like how you wanted it to look. But if God is calling you to move forward in that direction and it is in His will, you'll have peace. God will confirm it multiple times and in a load of unique ways. Remember that. Don't ever limit The Lord or put Him in a box. And when He *does* give us instructions, it's important to obey His timing. Ultimately, God knows when we are truly ready.

Scriptures: Ecclesiastes 3:1; Psalm 27:14;
Psalm 37:4; Psalm 46:10; Luke 16:10

Reference
- Riley Children's Health Indiana University Health. Understanding Scoliosis: How It Impacts the Body, Health & Wellness October 2024

Now we had talked with three different doctors before deciding to get the surgery. They told us that I was at risk of being paralyzed if I did not get it.

Because my curved spine was pushing down on my lungs, This intensified the asthma attacks as well. It seemed certain that if I got the surgery, it would greatly improve my lung health overall and reduce those attacks. I definitely needed and wanted that, but I stubbornly bucked against it for a while.

Although I had doubts about the surgery, I remember finally finding a potential surgeon that I actually liked and felt comfortable with. This was one of many ways God began sending confirmation that surgery was the right decision. I also started having dreams about how my future would look if I got the surgery. I clearly saw myself without a curved spine. In the dreams, I went on with life happily and in good health. In addition, I began randomly coming across others who had undergone the surgery. They shared their testimonies with me. The last bit of comfort I received was this powerful moment I had with my Heavenly Father.

One night, while I was again battling with the decision, a song dropped into my spirit out of nowhere. The song said, "Our God is mighty, mighty, mighty in all the earth/ He set the captives free/ He died for you and me." It kept ringing and ringing and ringing. This intrigued me. I couldn't believe it. I knew this was The Holy Spirit letting me know I was no longer going to be captive to this bodily infirmity. I had no reason to worry about how He would work to fix it.

After all this, my mind then changed. I felt more relaxed about the prospects of the surgery.

Scriptures: Philippians 4:7; Psalm 94:19; John 10:27-28; John 14:1— 3; John 14:27; John 16:13; Joshua 1:9; Proverbs 30:5; 2 Thessalonians 3:3

Encouragement, Advice, and Reflections

1. Dreams
2. The spine
3. Raised up

I remember once having a concerning dream early on about the surgery. I saw myself on the operating bed, and I almost died. This was one isolated negative dream surrounded by my other positive ones. I thought of this as confirmation not to move forward. But not every dream is from God. And sometimes it *can* be from Him, but we can misinterpret the message. Whenever you have a dream, pray over it to get the full meaning. Don't rely on your own interpretation.

The spine is crucial to the human body as it helps us perform many daily functions such as walking, sitting, standing, dancing, and more. It also gives shape and structure. The Devil wanted to attack my spine so that I wouldn't be able to stand up boldly and walk upright and so that I wouldn't be able to praise God through leaping and dancing, but no! My God was about to raise me up literally. I remember being informed that the procedure would improve my body's posture, which in turn would make me a few inches taller than I was. Ironically enough I had always desired to be taller, so this was a win for me! How could I turn down this offer? this was a true blessing in disguise! Improvement on design.

Imagine what a person would look like without a spine. Yikes.

To be spineless can mean different things from how we look at it. For instance, The Devil ultimately is "spineless," meaning he is weak and he has no true purpose, so there's no need to fear him. Amen! God is much higher than him, and so are we.

Scriptures: Genesis 50:20; Romans 4:17; Romans 8:11; Matthew 28:6; Acts 2:24-32; 1 Corinthians 6:14; 2 Corinthians 4:14-15; Philippians 3:21; 1 Peter 1:21; John 11:4; 2 Corinthians 5

So the plan was set for the summer, and honestly, in a way, I was feeling happy because I was ready for a change.

I envisioned how now I would truly be able to be fashionable. I would be able to wear cute clothes without seeing any malformation, I would basically have a whole new body!

Which in turn meant that I would be able to be absolutely as chic as I wanted. I would be able to go out to the mall and walk around looking good with no one staring or noticing my curved spine and asking questions. As my day for the surgery grew closer, my peace continued, and I had so much support. My auntie had bought me some new pajamas, slippers and my own towels and wash-cloths. They were very cute and fitting for me and comfy! Now I got my hair braided a few weeks beforehand so that I could rest afterward and not have to worry about it for a bit!

I remember that on July 10, 2007, I had woke up early on that very hot morning and I had my orders and followed them accordingly. I was told not to eat or drink anything. This is always a rule of thumb before every surgery. I remember exactly what I had put on that morning—a cute bright-green V-neck shirt, and I also wore these dark fitted denim jeans and these cute navy-blue wedge heels, I felt amazing! I was going in with style and faith.

Next, we arrived at the hospital early. It was me, my parents, and my little sister. We sat and waited for a few church members along with my older sister to arrive. After that, we all met with Dr. R. collectively and prayed. Amen! Honestly, this prayer session was very powerful, and it set the atmosphere.

Scriptures:1 John 5:14; Matthew 18:20; 1 Thessalonians 5:16—17; James 5:14—16

Afterward, I went in the back to get in my hospital gown and to get medicated.

My mom came with me. I remember them asking me which flavor I preferred.

They had two options—grape or bubble-gum. I chose the grape. I remember I could vividly taste it. This medication made me laugh hysterically.

Next thing I remember is waking back up in the operating room. It was dark inside, but they called my name and asked me to move my lower legs a bit, which was easy for me to do. Then I was rolled out.

I was still dozing a bit, but I was able to communicate properly. I had so much joy, which pleasantly baffled all, making me the talk of the town. Our Father tells us to do certain things because He knows and sees what we do not. Let this be a reminder: You can live your absolute best life no matter what situation you are in! On July 10, 2007 God made history. Glory Hallelujah!

Scriptures: Psalm 19:1; Psalm 100:4; Revelation 21:4-23; John 11:40; John 14:26; John 16:22; Romans 8:11–18; James 1:2; Galatians 5:22; Proverbs 10:22; Proverbs 17:22; Genesis 21:6

The surgery recreated me not just outwardly, but inwardly as well as it had required me to step outside of my comfort zone. Many times we think that we have faith, but it's actually just wishful thinking, or in some cases, idolatry. True faith requires full commitment to the very end, even when things get ugly. All in all, my prayer for a miraculous healing was answered. God performed it in an unorthodox way. Our God is a creative genius. Amen! Let Him have His way.

Scriptures: Isaiah 55:8—9; James 2:17

I felt no pain at all after the surgery, as I was on a ton of medication. I remember, particularly, morphine and a very strong Tylenol, but ultimately my strength came from God. Through Him, I had this miraculous and pain-free body.

Some churches that I attended advised against taking medication, stating that taking it means that one doesn't have faith, but again, God can work through everything. God is the one who gives the doctors the idea for the medicine to create. Due to Him making me so mighty, I wasn't bogged down in bed. I was able to swiftly get up and walk and move around. This continued to put all the hospital staff in utter wonder as they had expected me to be lying around and unable to do these things so effortlessly.

The goal of God from this surgery was to heal me, as well as spread a message of faith in Him. He wanted it to be known to everyone what He was capable of. He wanted that vividly showcased. I remember I had gotten so many cards with encouraging words; one card had mentioned this being God's handiwork. I remember a girl at the church, whom I was close friends with, designed for me this huge Hello Kitty Card. It was beautiful, I was a big fan back then. I had no clue that she was even doing it. My surgery was more of a celebration than anything.

My older sister felt moved by all that had taken place and wrote about me for one of her college classes. It was a beautiful paper that she put together. God poured out so many blessings for me through all of this!

Scriptures: Proverbs 17:17; Ecclesiastes 4:9— 12; Deuteronomy 15:11; John 15:27; Psalm 66:16; Revelation 12:11; 2 Timothy 1:8; Luke 4:18

I was put in my hospital room where I would be staying in for the next few days. I remember my mom was talking to me, and she was crying tears of joy. My mom was nervous before I had this surgery, as she had many concerns.

This was a release for her finally. God did the impossible! I remember she had gotten me a little something from the hospital gift store. It was a silver bracelet that had 2 Corinthians 5:7—"We walk by faith and not by sight"—engraved on it. It was beautiful!

My older sister arrived later that day after everything was completed. I remember when she arrived, she kissed me on my forehead. I then just got to lay in bed and sucked on a Popsicle and just overall chilled out. My mom, of course stayed with me the whole week I was there. I remember having a catheter bag in me, and I remember them removing it.

Afterward, I remember I struggled with some urine retention. Literally, I felt the urge to go, but I could not do it. The doctors turned on the water in the sink to set the mood for me, and eventually it did just that thankfully.

Encouragement, Advice, and Reflections

1. Purified and perfected
2. Jesus's surgery
3. Study word

During this time, I remember having very vivid dreams, and in one of my dreams, I had this bright orange hair. This may have seemed silly, but ironically enough, biblically, this color represents being purified and perfected under fire. This was true for me, My body had been purified and was perfected with The "Holy Ghost's fire," Amen!

Scriptures: 1 John 3:3; Hebrews 10:14; Hebrews 12:29; 2 Samuel 22:33—35

Jesus's crucifixion was basically like a surgery as well, and after all that took place, His body, as we know, was resurrected. The word *Resurrect* has two meanings: (1) to restore a dead person to life (2) to revive the practice, use, or memory of something. Synonyms of this word are *to revive, wake up*, and *reestablish*," Jesus's surgery was for us. We were dead people in sin, but He restored us to life. Amen!

I had many people come and visit me, but in a way, I didn't want them to because again, I didn't like attention. It is good to have support, but you also need to have discernment of who to let come around you. Some people have genuine intentions, others may not. Know the difference!

So the time finally came for me to leave. I remember the morning. I showered and put on some nice pajamas and a nice robe and slippers. My mom styled my hair a little bit, gathering my braids in a cute up-do using some butterfly ponytail holders, and I put on some lipstick. My dad came to pick us up. I remember he was pleased to see me dressed up like my usual self. I remember I had a huge long pillow for comfort and support for my back. When we arrived home, my parents planned on assisting me out of the car and into the house, but I had easily gotten up and out of the car on my own and walked up to the house all by myself. They were stunned.

Now, of course, the doctors gave me some orders to live by at home: I couldn't walk upstairs, and I couldn't take an actual bath, just a shower; but unfortunately, we didn't have one in the house at that time, But my mom figured out what to do. She had just bought a temporary shower-head. It was plastic and could be attached to the part of the tub where the water came out. This was a win. My mom bathed me every single day and night. I slept on the first floor with her and my little sister. Now one thing, though: Afterward, I had zero appetite, literally. I could eat only little by little, and certain things made me feel a bit nauseated due to this drastic change that my body had been through.

I remember I was craving some Sunchips, a specific flavor, so My mom and little sister went to go get them, but just my luck, no store had them. They looked everywhere. I wanted to scream. This couldn't be real!

The Devil was angry at how glorious my surgery was, and he still tried to attack me a bit during my recovery. I felt some shame still afterward. I felt a little down trying to get back to my normal, typical life. I just didn't feel the same in some ways. I remember that afterward, wearing clothes was very hard; I could wear only dresses, as they were all I felt comfortable in—literally no pants or anything else. I couldn't even wear a bra.

When I would go out in public places, I had to take a wheelchair with me, which I didn't want to do, and which made me feel embarrassed, like I wasn't truly healed and maybe should not have had the surgery and that it did more bad than good. I had lost tons of weight due to my loss of appetite, and people would comment on it. I remember when I returned to church, so many people expressed how much I had changed physically, but I couldn't help it. I felt very unattractive, so the comments only discouraged me more. Sighs. Looking at myself in the mirror haunted me. I started just wanting to stay inside; I didn't want to go out anymore.

Satan will try to sabotage our victory, but, we can't be moved by what we see or how we feel. Now, once the summer ended, of course I'd be going to high school, but there was some worry that I would need to delay high school after having this surgery. There was some talk about me potentially starting school a bit later, but no! I was one hundred percent very determined to fully get my life back. I wasn't going to stop. I had come way too far. I was young, so I *wasn't* going to not enjoy what was ahead of me. Firstly, with getting my appetite back, I would just force myself to eat. I would lie in bed on my back with my plate on my stomach and slowly finish eating all my food.

A few weeks later, I was back to normal. I was wearing all my cute clothes again. I was all ready to start high school! I still wanted to keep it on the low that I had surgery, though, but I remember that a few weeks before school actually started, I had to go up there to take a placement test, and I had to take my big long pillow for my back as I sat in that hard little seat. I felt so embarrassed, although there were only a few people in the room. I didn't want to draw any attention to myself at all!

Once the semester actually started, things weren't so easy. Per doctor's orders, I couldn't lift anything heavy or bend down. I remember my mom specifically got me a rolling book bag so I wouldn't have to carry anything heavy on my back. I would have to ask the other kids to pick stuff up for me. I hated it. No one teased me, but I didn't want to be asked questions or to have to explain my situation. Even telling my teachers bothered me, as I was always a very private person. I even took pain medication to school in a small little case. I remember one of my teachers would always let me get up and walk whenever my back would hurt. She would let me walk down to the water fountain to get a sip to take my meds.

Many things would trigger back pain, like when it rained in the morning, sometimes the pain made it hard for me to simply take out a milk gallon from the fridge, but again, my determination kept me going. Now at school, I remember they ended up making a rule that everyone could carry only a clear book bag for safety and security reasons, but I still couldn't carry anything on my back. So what was I going to do?

My mom gave me a big clear purse that she'd had for years. It was cute and different! I was well known for being unique and stylish; in fact, my nickname in high school was Ms. Exotic, so this clear-purse-turned-book-bag just allowed me to live up to my name. Things normally progressed for me regarding my back. I was glad and now lived like a normal teenager wearing my fly gear with a fully straight back. Amen!

Unfortunately, I still got stares afterward. The scar on my back was definitely noticeable. If I had a tank top or a tube top on, it could be seen, and the chatter would come. I remember one time at church: two older ladies sitting behind me noticed, and they worried that I had been physically abused, but I reassured them I was well and told them what really happened! But honestly, as of now, I am not ashamed of anyone noticing where I'd been cut because it shows that God imprinted His hand upon me through the doctor. Amen! This mark is fully straight. It's not crooked or anything. It's just right where it should be, nice and even. it's a forever reminder of my greatest victory. So people can stare all they want: This is my proof that The Lord can do all things!

Encouragement, Advice, and Reflections

1. Scars
2. Proof
3. Doubting Thomas
4. Give it back

Some people will believe only if they see things up close and personal. Jesus Himself had scars. If you're a believer, you may know about Thomas; but if you don't know, he had doubts and believed Jesus only by seeing, and even feeling, the holes in Him.

Scripture: John 20:24—27

I remember afterward, I found that my back brace was still in my closet, and I asked my mom what to do with it. She told me to throw it back to the pit of hell where it came from. Amen! Don't hold on to what God brought you out of. The past is over and not coming back.

Scripture: Galatians 5:1

Part 3: Skin Deep

I never knew that skin color mattered until I began to hear others refer to me as "brown skinned." Nowadays, society is different; Any shade of brown is celebrated and embraced in magazines, movies, and social media platforms.

Back then, though, lighter complexions were the only ones celebrated. And in my family, to the generation that my grandfather came from in the once deeply racist and segregated Southern area of Mississippi, darker skin was nothing to celebrate.

These negative perceptions of brown skin began to sink Into my own mind, and I started to become self-conscious of how I looked, even to the point where compliments from others had no impact on me. If I ever received them, I would often think the person was joking. I thought, *How could anyone perceive a quiet, browner skinned girl with "nappy hair" like me as beautiful?* I always wished for a silky hair texture and a lighter skin complexion as I thought that would make me as beautiful as ever, and all my insecurities would be completely gone. I would be that "it girl"—I'd really be popping. I remember when I was in middle school, I wrote a paper about if I had superpowers, and in my paper, I wrote that firstly, I would change how I looked, completely. Then I wrote that I would make myself light-skinned for a long period of time, and then lastly, I'd make myself dark-skinned too, but only for a short time. I remember my mom read my paper and told me that it sounded like low self-esteem, but I was in denial. didn't want to admit that I was having these problems.

I remember when I began wearing makeup—some people would tell me that I was "too dark" to wear the vivid colors which I loved and that I should only stick to wearing earth tone colors instead. Sigh.

"Nappy headed" is something that most of us heard while growing up. This was always associated with negativity. I never wanted my hair to be this way. I remember that as a child, I hated when my mom would wash my hair and it would scrunch up. I really thought negatively of my hair back then. To fix things, I ended up getting my first hair perm at the age of nine, which made my hair texture silky, just like I badly ever so wanted, so I finally thought that I was beautiful for a little while; however, my feelings of inadequacy regarding my appearance eventually returned.

Because I didn't have the light skin and silky hair that I desired, my dream was that when I grew up, I would have a daughter who would be light-skinned with silky hair. This was silly thinking.

Once I had gotten older, particularly in my late teens and early twenties, I embraced my natural hair and started wearing it all on its own—no chemical straightening at all. I would proudly rock what I once wanted to hide, and I would get so many nice compliments. My hair, I now know, isn't nappy. It's beautifully abundant. I haven't had any chemical processes on it in years.

I have had issues with hair loss, but every time, God always restored my hair vigorously. Amen!

I have also start embracing my skin by simply keeping it healthy, not even focusing on its color and I still proudly rock my vivid colored makeup which I know I look good in.

Encouragement, Advice, and Reflections

1. Love yourself
2. How God sees us
3. Healing of hair and skin
4. Thick hair
5. We're all unique
6. Embrace yourself
7. No division
8. Don't change

Love the skin that you are in. Firstly, understand this: our bodies are just a covering, a shell, but not who we really are or how we really look. God sees us much differently. Next, understand it's a blessing to have skin and hair period; especially healthy skin and hair, we take the little things for granted. Maybe you are reading my book and your hair has fallen out due to some illness, I promise you, The Lord is going to restore it back ten fold. Amen! You may have a skin ailment. The Father is restoring that outer layer and keeping it healthy and intact. You will testify. I speak life to your body, and you will glisten with glory. Amen!

Please remember this God created every part of us, when we insult ourselves or even someone else we are insulting His creation. A full scalp is a sign of good health and nothing broken or missing. The truth is that many people desire to have a coily texture. Understand this, silky hair is beautiful no doubt, but there's certain styles that may not take well with it. Coily hair often allows for more versatility with hairstyles; you can braid it, twist it, loc it etc. I'm not shaming you if you're reading my book and you only have a fine grade of hair, but I'm just saying to those reading who were like myself. Yes it's okay to straighten your hair texture at times. I like sleekness for certain events, but I am no longer ashamed of what I was born with! When we were created, every little detail was put together perfectly. Ladies and Gentlemen Embrace what God gave you! Love the skin you're in and love what is up on top of your head!

Scriptures: Proverbs 31:30; Psalm 139:14; 1 Samuel 16:7; Genesis 1:27; 1 Corinthians 11:15; 2 Corinthians 4:18; John 7:24; Luke 12:7; Luke 21:18; Revelation 1:14—16; Judges 16:17

God doesn't make no junk! Everyone is unique; we are all different, yet in the eyes of The Lord, we are all the same. The Bible says that there should not be any division among us, The Body Of Christ. We should not divide each other by race, gender, etc. If you ever considered someone different from you due to any of this or called someone a racist name, even if it was in a joking manner, please rethink what you say and how you view others. We are to esteem our brother or sister as better than ourselves.

Scriptures: Galatians 3:28; 1 John 4:20; 1 Corinthians 1:10; 1 Thessalonians 5:11; Ephesians 4:29; Hebrews 10:24—25; Romans 2:11; Romans 14:19; Romans 15:2; Proverbs 27:17;Matthew 22:36—40

I had been teased by this boy for having "thick, hairy eyebrows." This was true for me. I always had thick brows, which affected my self-esteem, so the comments really bothered me a lot. When I got home, I attempted to shave my brows down to a thinner size to improve my appearance, but I used an actual razor for body hair, and I ended up just messing up my brows quite badly. "Yikes." I was worried about my mom finding out, so I cut some hair off one of my baby dolls and glued it onto my brow area so my mom wouldn't notice.

Bad idea! She saw very clearly, and she was furious, but she had no idea about the teasing I was enduring. However, to fix things, she took me to get the proper tools to trim facial hair. She and my older sister carved everything down evenly, and I was satisfied. My mom approved of me to keep this new look we had achieved. So I was happy and felt somewhat prettier. Yet the next day, nothing changed. The boy still teased me. Moral of the story: Never change yourself for another person! Accept you for you—flaws and all.

Scripture: Galatians 1:10

References
- The 'Melaniin Goddess': Meet the model whose skin tone made her a social media sensationCNN updated 6:02 AM EST, Thu January 31, 2019.
- We Need To Talk About Colorism in The Black Community," March 21, 2023

Part 4: Weightless

"Watch what you eat!"
"Keep your weight down!"
"Don't get fat."
"It's harder to lose weight once you get older."

These were the thoughts and phrases that often plagued my mind when I would eat. My mom, my aunts, and the women at church would often jokingly say these things, not even knowing how much I was actually taking them to heart.

I remember once, when I was eleven years old, one of my aunts had told me that I had gotten fat. The memory is very clear. I had on a green two-piece outfit, and though self-esteem was such a struggle for me, I felt somewhat pretty in this outfit. Now she repeatedly commented on my weight the whole, entire time she was at the house. For years after, she would encourage me not to gain any more weight. Throughout my life, certain medications would involuntarily make my weight fluctuate.

At first, I didn't think too much about these comments, until years later.

Right before starting my last year of high school, I grew more conscious of my body weight, and I started to change my diet little by little and exercising a little more. It got extreme, though, to the point where I skipped meals some days drinking only water. I remember one day I drank water all day at school, and I was peeing all day, but my pee was water, my urine was clear, yet I thought I was doing my body justice. I remember my family went to a burger restaurant, and I just got a salad and water, nothing else. I was scared of gaining weight. I had to keep a fit body in my mind. I would also exercise after every meal to avoid gaining weight. I had become a perfectionist with this because I simply believed I needed to be perfect in every area of my life, including my weight and my body. Now, the eating disorder I was wrestling with wasn't anorexia nervosa, as I never threw up my food, but it was still a very restrictive diet with excessive exercise, which was still unhealthy.

Encouragement, Advice, and Reflections

1. More than a number on a scale
2. Types of eating disorders
3. Body positivity
4. Healthy eating
5. Glorify God
6. Different shapes and sizes
7. Support system

Eating disorders among teenage girls and young women are very common, unfortunately. But let's be honest—we live in a world that's obsessed with size, which makes it very easy to get caught up trying to achieve outward perfection, and it's a fact that teenage girls and young women have high rates of eating disorders or are at risk of developing eating disorders. Now eating disorders can affect teenage boys and young men as well, but they are more prevalent among females. There are many different types of eating disorders: anorexia nervosa, bulimia, binge eating, etc. Eating disorders are very dangerous; although dieting seems beneficial, when not done right, it is a form of harm to the body and can even cause death. Yikes.

We should be mindful of what we say to children regarding their weight, and we should model healthy eating and exercise habits:It is good to eat healthy and exercise, but it should be in moderation; healthy eating doesn't mean limiting or throwing up food after eating. It's important to talk to children about positive body image. Never joke with a child by calling them fat or chubby. Build a child's body confidence by calling them beautiful and encouraging them to be active—not to lose weight, but to be active to enjoy life and to grow strong! It's also okay to eat certain foods in moderation, such as fast food and sweets, but you don't have to restrict those things completely. Love your body and feed it when it's hungry. Weight gain isn't all bad; there is healthy weight gain.

God created our bodies for His glory, not even for our own. We are to glorify God in our body by taking care of it. Healthy food consists of protein, lean meats, nuts, healthy fats. Yes, some fat is healthy, such as polyunsaturated, monounsaturated fats found in fruits and vegetables.

Understand this: God created all of us differently. We are all different shapes and sizes, and that's what makes us unique. Each body type is beautiful; it would be so boring if everyone had the same body type. Embrace whatever size you are, women—and even any men reading who dislike the size of their body.

Reference
- American Academy Of Child and Adolescent Psychiatry.Eating Disorders in Teens updated March 2018.

Eventually, my eating disorder went away, and I didn't care too much whether or not if I gained weight, and I didn't exercise much at all. Years later, I found out about a group for those who were struggling with an eating disorder or who had an eating disorder in the past, and I decided to join this group. It was during the week, during the evening hours, I went and shared my story and met a few other women. The group was very comforting! It felt good to talk and not be in denial anymore, to have no more shame and to realize there were other people like me who struggled in the same area. In this group, it was very intimate. Some girls would cry, but there was full support and listening with zero judgement. The Bible says we are to carry the burden of others. Whatever size you are, you're beautiful. Let no one tell you otherwise. I myself, as of now, I exercise twice a week—not to avoid gaining weight but for my heart health and for strength; and I try to eat healthy meals and snacks as much as possible, but I don't restrict my diet anymore. Go ahead, gobble up ya favorite meal with no shame, and it's okay if you miss some exercise days. All in all, God will persevere our bodies, no matter what!

Scripture: Galatians 6:2

Part 5: Academics

In school, I was a mostly C student. I rarely got A's, so I felt that I wasn't smart. I tried my best, but still my report card was always the same, covered in C's. Sigh. This discouraged me greatly. I desired to be a better student. As we all know, A's are very good. Things came so naturally to others, but not me. Not being the best made me want to throw in the towel. I was good in only a couple areas.

I tried my absolute best, but still nothing. Sigh. I desired to make the honor roll, but that seemed impossible.

To stay somewhat afloat in school, I was put in a special education class, which only embarrassed me and made me feel like a complete loser. Sigh. I was also very quiet, which didn't help me either. I absolutely hated it when teachers would pick me to read aloud or go up to the board. I wished for a bold personality; I wished I was more confident to do tasks like I would see others do, but I would be sitting way in the back of the classroom trying to avoid being noticed. One benefit of my quiet personality; I was always praised and even rewarded for great behavior. I longed to be praised regarding my academics though. I envisioned if my report card had all A's, I'd be so ecstatic.

I made a few A's every now and then, but literally, it would be limited to say, just one to two, that's it. I longed for bigger milestones. I would always get super excited when I would get any type of certificate, and I would save it as it made me feel like I was a top dog. But I would feel so low due to all that I lacked.

This weighed heavy on how I viewed myself, and I worried about my future and potential prospects. I remember that as a high school freshman, my GPA was 2.1, which is considered not so good. Even to do certain school activities, you had to have at least a 2.5.

Mine stayed under that. It was always between 2.1-2.3 only. Sigh. I did all my work and tried my absolute best. Now, I remember when I was in the tenth grade, I was failing chemistry greatly. I had a 7% F. Yikes. I was going to potentially need summer school, as the school semester would be ending within a few weeks. There wasn't much that I could do. I was so shaken up, I texted my mom. She just prayed, as always. She didn't scold or punish me about this. I remember the teacher told me there was one way to redeem myself, and that was through writing this paper. I can't exactly remember what it was about, but I do remember I just went my absolute hardest on it. I prayed as well. I wanted to live my life with no problems; it was now or never at this point. I wrote that paper so extensively and handed it to the teacher. She didn't seem so convinced, though. I remember she fussed at me when we initially talked about where I was in her class, but hey, faith of a mustard seed. Nothing is too hard for Him above, and no situation we face is unimportant. The Bible says cast your cares on Him because He cares. Our Lord is all about favor!

Weeks later, I didn't think too much about the situation. I had peace. So school ended. I remember my last day of tenth grade vividly. I wore a bright, colorful silky-material shirt and a sequin denim skirt and some retro funky platform shoes. It was just a half day, but I had fun! Weeks after, I still felt at ease and was unworried about whether I was going to have my summer interrupted. I remember that finally, my report card had came in the mail. My mom got it, and I had got slight anxiousness in my stomach. She opened it. I remember vividly that she was sitting on the couch, and she looked at it and then handed it to me. I saw that I had passed chemistry with a C and the teacher wrote a little note on the side telling me to have a great summer. Amen! God had pulled me through. He's always on time! He fights for us, yet I still struggled academically the next year. Sigh. I didn't think too much about it, though. All I could do was my best.

However, by the end of my junior year, I got a pleasant surprise. I had shockingly made the honor roll! Now, funny I wasn't even at school on this particular day, but a friend of mine called and notified me that my name had been called up during a ceremony for the candidates. I was super shocked. I had even stopped thinking about everything and was actually content with where my grades were, but our Father in Heaven has the final say. He knew my long-awaited hope. If we delight ourselves in Him, He will give us the desires of our heart. Amen!

Everything is in His timing, Although I didn't make the list exactly when I wanted to, I made it just at the opportunity that was handpicked for me!

The Devil doesn't like it when we have any victory whatsoever, and he will try to take us back to what we were brought out of, making it seem as though we aren't truly free.

Eventually, I fell off again during my last year of high school. The C's came back, and I was even failing in a class.

We all can relate to how school in this area can be very stressful. The thoughts come into your mind. *What am I going to do? What will my parents say? How will this impact my future?*

Especially with me being a senior, it wasn't a joke. It was critical that my grades needed to be top-notch, even with applying to college, most of the time, they look at your transcripts. So yeah, something had to be done. I didn't have much time. Talk about major stress.

Thankfully, all paid off. I remember I literally I ended up back on track just a few short months before graduation. I had gotten a 3.3 GPA Wow! I was so happy I kept looking at it, amazed. I had ended up staying on the honor roll, all the way up till the day that I graduated. Amen!

Though this was a small, and to most people probably a typical achievement, it was special to me. The sovereign Lord cares about every detail of our lives, even the tiniest things! Nothing is wasted. He knows our beginning and our end!

Encouragement, Advice, and Reflections

1. You can do all things through Christ
2. A helper
3. Take your time
4. Your future
5. Favor in school
6. Not too late

If you're a teen or a college student reading my book, you can do it! If no one ever told you, including your teachers, peers, even your very own parents, I assure you that you can! The Bible says we can do all things through Christ and that we are more than conquerors through Him. If you're stressed about school, relax. God will get you through as He did with me. Our worth doesn't come from our achievements—not that there's anything wrong with achievements or wanting to achieve, but our true worth comes from God. Keep that in mind, God loves you no matter what GPA you have. Don't limit success just to good grades alone; success is also peace, joy (contentment), a strong relationship with God, good physical health, being safe, and alive. To those in high school, I must say this: Do not limit yourself to just going to college. There is nothing wrong with going to college; however, college may not be where everyone is called to go. God made all of us unique, with different interests and talents for a reason. Don't try to live the dream of someone else. Be you—that's it!

Reference
- Anna Davies "Why College May Not Be for Everyone" 9 minute read SoFi Learn September 14, 2023.

There is no shame in having to get or ask for help. God gave us a helper—The Holy Spirit. He is a 24/7 tutor. He's always available no matter what time of day. He can give us all the answers we need so that we won't fail in any area of our life. Amen!

Scriptures: Jeremiah 33:3; Genesis 2:18; Psalm 121:3—5

Becoming a stellar student truly takes time. As mentioned, I didn't make the honor roll exactly when I had wanted to, but in due time, I did. Even if you are studying consistently, good things still take time. Everyone's brain processes information differently, but patience is key! Don't be too hard on yourself; instead, be patient with yourself!

Your future is in God's hands! Your teachers may try to speak negatively against your future, but they can't stop the future that God has planned for you. Your teachers may put you down or tell you that you don't have the skills to live out your dreams. Drown out the negative voices so that you can hear "The One Above." I had some teachers try to speak over my future, but ha! Look at me now! Remember who is your Maker. You will be everything that you were called to be and more in Jesus's name. Amen! The battle has already been won! Remember, failure is not final. Even if your bad grades are because of poor decisions, such as skipping school, not studying, etc. The Father will still have mercy on you. You can never mess up so bad that He won't love you. He is our advocate. Amen! Even with difficult teachers, God softens hearts. You will have favor all throughout school, I decree and declare.

Scriptures: Micah 7:18; John 14:12; 1 John 2:1; Psalms 138:8; Ecclesiastes 9:11; Deuteronomy 28:13; Hebrews 10:35—37; Hebrews 12:1; Amos 9:13—15; Galatians 6:9; Matthew 20:16

Even if you are someone who didn't complete high school, you are still worthy and can do all that God has planned for you. If you're someone who desires to go back to school, it's not too late.

Part 6: I'm rubber, You're Glue.

It's no secret we all know what a bully is and may have experienced being bullied at one point or another in our lives, whether in childhood, or even in adulthood. Truthfully, bullies can be at any age, they never fully go away. Now, some of us may refer to bullies as "Haters." We've heard many phrases such as "You not doing nothing special if you don't have haters," or "haters are just confused admirers." Well, that's actually true. Most individuals who pick on others don't truly dislike that person. These people often have their own issues that they are trying to confront, and they do so by lashing out at others. That's the only way they know how to handle things. This is seen so often. Bullies are often in school and the workplace—-unfortunately, even in families.

Think of the story of Joseph in The Bible. Please study this story. His brothers were so jealous of him that they sold him into slavery. Also, study the story of Cain and Abel; Cain's jealousy made him kill his brother Abel. "Yikes."

Jealousy can get very deep; it's an issue that needs to be thoroughly dealt with.

Scriptures: Proverbs 14:30; Genesis 4; Genesis 37:18—36

I remember a situation I found myself in, in school—grade eight, to be exact.

Now, in school, although I was quiet, I was still fairly approachable and could mix well with just about anyone. A girl and I quickly formed a relationship, but one problem! She was quite unkind. She would always comment negatively on my hair. I always kept my hair together and was creative with it. Though my family didn't have loads of money, I knew how to look good on a budget. This girl wore her hair in only one style—a basic ponytail with loads of gel. Her hair was a bit thin, might I add, hence she was jealous of mine. When people say mean things to you it's actually them projecting their own feelings of inferiority onto you to take the heat off of themselves. This girl also lived in the projects, which a project for the most part is smaller than a house and has less amenities than a house or even an apartment. Now although my family wasn't living in the projects, we weren't exactly living in a mansion. See, many times the person that you are jealous of is struggling just as you are.

You just think they may have it better, but little do you know. This girl would even beg for food at lunchtime, as she probably didn't have much to eat at home. Now I don't recall her having many friends or being that popular at the school; she mainly flocked under me.

Clearly, loneliness was an issue that she was facing, and she wanted friendship, but didn't know what a healthy friendship was. This girl ended up stealing from me—a purse, to be exact. Now, I myself never valued material things like that; however, I ended up getting my purse back, with some help, of course. But the bullying continued. I was never mean back to this girl; I always was a non-confrontational individual, and truthfully, her ways didn't bother me too much. I was mostly able to ignore her. It really bothers a bully when they can't get under your skin as they would like.

As believers, how should we handle bullies? Should we tolerate disrespect? Well, the Bible has lots to say about this issue, but understand this: God does not expect us to tolerate mistreatment. We can indeed set appropriate boundaries.

However, we should also look at people through the eyes of God. It was quite evident that this girl was facing multiple issues and, in turn, looking for some way out unknowingly. This girl wasn't present during our eight-grade dinner dance; her mother probably was unable to afford to buy her a dress, or ultimately just didn't want to, as there appeared to be neglect.

At graduation, the girl was present, and so was her mom, but the mom seemed zoned out and barely paid the girl much attention. I remember that on this day, her mother was wearing an old and too-little skirt and just walking very discombobulated. "Yikes." After eighth grade, I didn't keep in contact with this girl, but I remember seeing on Facebook that she had became a teen mom.

Hopefully, all worked out for her and her child, and that this big life event had changed her for the better. Now understand that forgiveness is not excusing toxic behavior—it's being mature and wise enough to move forward. Even if no apology ever comes, though sometimes it will, unfortunately, many times, people don't even recognize the harm that they are doing to others.

However, at the same time, we can become fed up with continual mistreatment, and in this case, we should seek out professional, or even legal help if a situation is too chaotic and if a person refuses to respect our boundaries.

There is also even nothing wrong with distancing yourself from someone who doesn't treat you well. Let God lead you on what to do if you find yourself in this type of situation.

Scripture: Luke 23:34

Reference
- Health-directBullying10-minute read

Encouragement, Advice, and Reflections

1. Recognizing a bully
2. The perpetrator
3. Battle fighter
4. Speak the truth
5. Unlikely friends
6. Laughing at your bully
7. Don't let your issues define you
8. Standing up for someone
9. David and Goliath

What does a bully look like? Well, in most shows and movies, bullies are portrayed as bigger than the victim, and they may often dress a certain way. The girl who was bullying me was actually smaller than I was, shockingly. Signs of impending bullying can be simply a person taking from you, or even a person controlling you, trying to change you. This was somewhat seen in my situation as she commented negatively on my hair. Her doing so meant she was probably thinking it would discourage me and make me change my hair. But no, let no one change you!

Maybe you are someone who isn't being bullied but is the actual bully. Perhaps this is your way to try to cope with the hell that surrounds you. Well, good news. You don't have to pick on others. All you have to do is surrender your problems to God. He loves you! Love yourself so that you can know how to properly love others.

To those who are bullied, you can rest assured that God will, indeed, fight your battles for you. He is a just God. To parents: if you discover that your child is being bullied, try to handle it with a level head. I remember my mom was furious about this incident and wanted to snap, but I encouraged her to handle it smoothly.

Scripture: Deuteronomy 32:35

Though it's way easier said than done, Pray for them. Pray for their eyes to be opened. Amen! They're being used by Satan and don't even know it. However, don't be afraid to face a bully—meaning, tell them how you feel, even if they aren't receptive. At least you were honest, and they may get it eventually. Ask God to give you the courage and the words to say to them. I had another bullying incident in high school. However, I had confronted this person, and they were not receptive at all. In fact, they got mad and started crying; hence they knew they were wrong, but didn't want to admit it. Pride is often what most bullies have. This person did speak to me at prom, though, but no further contact after that. Many times, God will just make peace, and that will be that.

Can a bully eventually change their ways and become your friend? As odd as this sounds, yes, indeed. There's been many cases of this. I remember even watching a few shows where this happened. Never doubt what God can do and who He can use. It may seem unbelievable, but He can change even the worst person on the planet; however, always have discernment and seek God's counsel before rekindling any relationship.

If you grew up in the '90s like myself, then you are probably well familiar with the Nickelodeon, and later Disney, cartoon

Doug. In this cartoon, the bully was *Roger Klotz*; however I remember Doug wasn't even scared of Roger and always faced him. In fact, everyone did; he even got punched in the stomach in one episode—proof that bullies are truly weak but try to portray a tough exterior. I remember Roger eventually becoming cool with Doug and there being minimal drama. Doug even helped him quite a few times. Doug was the bigger person. Bullies generally aren't on your level maturity-wise, so set the example. Don't stoop to their level.

What about when your bully falls? As mentioned in my story on how the girl's life turned out, well, it may be really tempting to rejoice when a bully falls into their own woes, which, most of the time, they do. However, The Bible says a lot about this as well—it advises against it, actually. Instead, pray for them still. Pray for their mercy. Much easier said than done, I know, but ultimately the best thing to do.

Scripture: Proverbs 24:17—18

Ultimately, people have issues that they can't help. A person can't help what situation they were born into, and this situation can negatively or positively affect them. This girl was clearly from a bad situation that was out of her control, but hopefully, as she grew up, she decided to make a change and not let what she was born into define her. The Devil wants people to stay in bondage to their situation, but no, God has freedom for us. Don't let your situation make you bitter, jealous, and mean. Use it as fuel to do better. Everyone on earth has issues, but it's what they choose to do with their issues.

What about standing up for someone you see being bullied? Some may advise against this, especially if it's a dangerous situation. If the situation looks too dangerous to intervene, don't hesitate to call the police instead. But all in all, pray if it's meant for you to intervene, The Holy Spirit will lead you in what to do and say and He will give you courage and confidence.

Scriptures: Proverbs 31:8– 9; Isaiah 42:7— 9; Ephesians 6:12; Matthew 5:44; Hebrews 12:14

Lastly, you may know the story in The Bible about David and the giant Goliath. Literally, David was small, and Goliath was huge, but David didn't fear him and ultimately defeated him. Even if your bully is bigger than you, there's no need to be afraid.

Scriptures: 1 Samuel 17; 1 John 4:4; Luke 10:19

CHAPTER SIX
A YOUNG MIND ATTACKED

Warning! (Viewer discretion advised) In this chapter, there will be discussion about mental health. If you are someone who lost a loved one to suicide, my honest condolences to you. Please, if suicide is a triggering topic for you, I advise you to skip reading this chapter of my book, because this chapter contains discussion of suicide and mental illness. In this chapter, I am not trying to give you any answers about your loved one who committed suicide. I will just share my personal journey in this area, and I am more so specifically speaking to those who are living and having thoughts of suicide!

Scripture: Proverbs 4:23

It's no secret, the importance of mental health. This is a serious issue, and lately, it's become less of a stigma than in the past, which is very good.

There are many different mental health issues a person can have such as depression, anxiety, and suicidal thoughts.

Depression is defined as a mood disorder that causes a persistent feeling of sadness. Although depression and sadness can be similar, depression is different. It's more extreme and lasts longer than sadness. Sadness may last for a few hours or a few short days; depression lasts for weeks, months, or even years. Yikes. Depression causes loss of interest. Depression affects how a person thinks, feels, or behaves. It can disrupt normal day-to-day activities and can make you feel as though life isn't worth living. If you are depressed, you may not want to leave your house or go anywhere. You may sleep a lot or sometimes not at all. You may eat a lot or lose your appetite completely. You also may not shower or bathe. However, there's some people that are depressed can still easily do their usual day-to-day activities, but that's usually a way of blocking things out, some people try to fight depression by keeping busy. There are certain risk factors for depression, such as genetics. If depression is just in your family. The Devil likes to attack families, he likes to keep things going for years to come. Depression can be a generational curse—say, if everyone in your family battled depression and then it comes to you. We have the power to break generational curses; we have the authority to say, "it stops here—My life will be different."

Chronic stress can cause depression; a traumatic experience; grief, such over losing a loved one; and your environment can all be factors of depression. There's also postpartum depression among women, or even depression during pregnancy that some women suffer—prenatal depression. This can be due to all the new hormones or a stressful pregnancy experience, lack of support, etc.

Now with depression can come anxiety. What is anxiety? It is excessive, persistent worry or dread. Anxiety can affect your body. You may sweat, or your heart may be faster than usual. You may be unable to breathe easily, or you may feel nauseated, and may even vomit.

Anxiety may make it hard for you to fall asleep or stay asleep.

Scripture :Proverbs 3:24

Feeling down at times doesn't mean you lack faith—you're still human. While here on earth, Jesus felt all that we felt; He lived in a human body and had human thoughts and emotions. The Bible is clear on taking our thoughts captive.

It's not a sin to be depressed or anxious however, that's not God's will for us. He has given us power over these things, while Jesus was on earth, though He went through all that we went through, He never gave in or quit.

I have struggled with both depression and anxiety in my life, and it was for a long period. I didn't understand it at first, though. I remember at times that I would feel very anxious early in my life, between the ages of nine through twelve particularly, sometimes it would be very hard for me to relax. My mind would just fill with thoughts of scary things. I could be playing with my friends or siblings, cousins, and still those thoughts would be on my mind, and they would also keep me up all night. I didn't know how to get them to stop. These thoughts would go into overdrive. I'd be in bed feeling extremely uneasy for no particular reason that I knew of.

Parents, please, if your child is having anxious or scary thoughts, or even constant nightmares, please take this seriously. It's not just normal things that children go through—it's an early spiritual attack on the mind, and this can be linked to the child's mental health as well. Anxiety, depression, and other mental health conditions can cause nightmares. Know that The Devil will try as early as possible, and it all starts in the mind. Nightmares can also contribute negatively to mental health causing anxiety, PTSD, and more. When you have a nightmare, it may make you anxious, or cause your heart to beat fast, it can trigger sweating and heavy breathing, etc.

Reference
- Shah Yusra Nightmare Disorder: Why Do I Keep Having Bad Dreams? Reviewed by April Kilduff, MA, LCPC, NOCDAugust 23, 2024 (10-minute read).

I remember being super anxious one night when I was twelve. It was quite scary. I remember sitting on the couch extremely overwhelmed, feeling as though I was going to have a breakdown or a panic attack. I didn't understand why. It was very uncomfortable. Yikes.

Depression and anxiety can also come with thoughts of suicide. I had my first thought of suicide at age twelve, but I immediately knew it wasn't God speaking to me. This thought left and didn't return until five years later. This time it was more detailed. The thought was to commit suicide and to do so by slitting the side of my neck with a knife. Yikes. Again, I knew this wasn't God.

No more thoughts until a few years later into my early adulthood. The thought was to do so by overdosing on Benadryl pills as they will knock you straight out, putting you into a deep sleep rather quickly.

Scripture: 1 Peter 5:8

There are some individuals who are at risk. These individuals have higher suicide rates than others, unfortunately.

Teens and young adults, males, LGBT individuals, and older adults.

When it comes to the teens and young adults The Devil desires to take people out early before their purpose fully starts. When you're young, you have so much ahead of you. The Devil knows this and desires to cut it short or stop it completely. I know this is why Satan attacked me so much early on, but God!

Parents, please talk to your children about mental health. If they show signs of depression, anxiety, or suicide ideation, if they express that they have suicidal thoughts, please take it seriously. Don't judge them or downplay how they feel.

Reference
- The Jed Foundation, Mental Health and Suicide Statistics

When it comes to high suicide rates amongst the males, if you're a believer, you probably know the story about King Herod, but if you don't know, I will put the scripture down below for you to read, but long story short, King Herod wanted all the males age two and under to be killed. It's no secret that The Devil attacks the men so hard. Men are often leaders and the head of their homes which is the reason why The Devil desires to take them out.

Scripture: Matthew 2:13-16

It's no secret that The Devil wanted Jesus dead. He thought that when Jesus died on the cross, that was it and thought he had won, but little did he know. The Bible says, "Don't touch my anointed ones." Amen! If you have a son, please pray for him daily, pray for his mind, pray he grows up to become the man God intended for him to be—"the mighty man of valor." Pray for your husband, brother, nephew, male friends, etc. Pray over every single male that you know!

Reference
- Hinch Will: "Why are suicides so high amongst men? Priory
- Three-quarters of all suicides involve men. We explore the reasons behind the suicide gap.

Nothing against LGBT individuals however, lifestyle is a factor in mental health—which is the reason why God wants to save the LGBT community. If you are an LGBT individual reading my book, God doesn't hate you. He loves you. Come to Him!

Reference
- Newport Academy. "New Research on LGBTQ + Teen Suicide Rates."
- UCLA School of Law, Williams Institute. "More than 60% of suicide attempts among LGBQ people happen within five years of realizing they are LGBQ," Press release.

Older adults have higher rates of suicide. The Devil desires to stop them from making it to the finish line. It would be horrible to make it to seventy, eighty, ninety or one hundred years old, only to then just throw in the towel. No way!

God has brought you a long way; it's a blessing to live that long. Heaven is cheering you on to finish strong. Amen!!

Scripture: Hebrews 12:1

Reference
- National Council on Aging. "Suicide and Older Adults: What You Should Know,"
- Depression and Anxiety. January 3, 2025 (6-minute read).

Encouragement, Advice, and Reflections

1. Truths
2. Life planned
3. Increase and completion
4. God's voice or not

5. Past Over-comers
6. The Devil is a liar
7. God's true plan
8. Power in actions
9. No creation in vain
10. Support

We all know what murder is and that it can be committed in many different forms either subtle or aggressive. But most of us mainly think of murder in just one way, such as murdering another person with a weapon. That's it, right? Well, no, murder can be more complex.

Scriptures: Exodus 20:13; Proverbs 6:16—17

Committing suicide is essentially similar to getting an abortion, as both involve voluntarily taking a life, which in turn stops a family line from growing and continuing. People often commit both of these acts because they don't see any positive ways to make it through. There are many ways to get an abortion; there are many ways to commit suicide. Yikes.

Now if you're reading this chapter and you had an abortion, I am not judging you by any means; I'm just giving some insight. Please forgive yourself. I understand that some people are forced to get an abortion, so if that's your situation, I understand, and I am sorry you had to experience that.

Reference
- Kissen, Debra 13 Reasons Why Suicide Is a Bad Idea" Light on anxiety treatment center April 18.
- Lantz, Len. A Note to the Suicidal Christian.

We are to live by faith not fear; uncertainty.

Scripture: Romans 1:17

God already has our life planned out. His ways and timing are different than ours. Before conception even happened at all, you existed. Even if your parents didn't plan on having you, God did! He makes no mistakes, You are His child.

Scripture: Jeremiah 1:5

Suicide, just like abortion, is not directly mentioned in The Bible, but even if a topic isn't mentioned specifically, does it line up with God's character and His principles? There lies your answer.

Scriptures:1 Thessalonians 5:22—24; Proverbs 14:12

God is full of increase!
Scriptures: Psalm 115:14—15; Job 8:7; 1 Corinthians 3:6— 8; Genesis 1:28; Malachi 3:8— 10; Isaiah 61:7— 8; Joel 2:25

God completes what He starts; everything He made on earth, He did not undo it after it's completion.

One church that I attended, the pastor said, "Don't put a period where God has a comma. One of my aunts always said she believes that a true believer won't take their life no matter how bad it gets. "A true believer would pull through." In The Bible there are many real stories of people who made it through. Think of Job. If you're a believer, you probably know his story, but if not, long story short, he lost everything, but he didn't end his life. His own wife wanted him to curse The Lord. Literally, she said, "Curse your God and die," but he refused. Amen!

Scripture: Job 2:9—10

There are many scriptures in The Bible about being steadfast, unmoved.

Scriptures: 1 Corinthians 15:58; Psalm 136:1—26; James 1:2— 4; Lamentations 3:22—23

One church that I attended had did a skit about people struggling with different things. In one of the skits there was a young guy who was struggling with suicidal thoughts. An evil voice told him to kill himself, and, unfortunately, he obeyed, shooting himself with a gun.

I remember I was friends with this lady who was also struggling with some mental health issues. She had once heard a voice say to her, "B—— kill yourself." Yikes. Fortunately, she didn't obey this voice. God is a God of encouragement; He will never discourage you, remember that!

Scripture: John 10:27—28

The Devil is a liar; he likes to twist the truth. Understand that he will try to disguise what the word really means. If you read in the book of Genesis, you will see that he did this with Adam and Eve in the garden of Eden. Unfortunately, they both obeyed him, and things turned out bad for them. If God tells us something, it's for a good reason.

Scriptures: John 8:44; 2 Thessalonians 2:3

Ultimately, death was never a part of God's plan for mankind. This is why He made it where we can have eternal life in Heaven. He doesn't desire us to die physically or spiritually, although physical death is real, mostly unavoidable. You don't have to be old or sickly to die; however, God desires us to live. Amen!

Scriptures: John 3:16; John 8:51; John 10:10; John 11:25; John 14; 1 John 5:4; 3 John 1:2; Psalm 56:8; Psalm 91:16; Psalm 118:17; Psalm 139:16; 1 Corinthians 6:20, 1 Corinthians 10:13;1 Corinthians10:23; 1 Corinthians 13:7; 2 Corinthians 4:8-9; 2 Corinthians 4:16-18; 2 Corinthians 10:5; 2 Corinthians 12:9; James 1:12; Leviticus 19:28; Malachi 3:11; Proverbs 4:23—27, Proverbs 17:22; Romans 8:28; Proverbs 3:7; Proverbs 16:31; Philippians 4:8; Philippians 4:13;Galatians

6:9; Jeremiah 29:11;Proverbs 18:21; Ephesians 4:27—30; Isaiah 65:20;Mark 11:23; Matthew 11:28—30;Psalm 94:19

When we are going through bad times, we don't really want to be dead—we just want to be out of the bad situation that we're in. Understand the difference. Please don't let The Devil deceive you into believing that dying is your only option just because of a bad *temporary* situation. The Devil will try to get us to magnify our problems. Everything in life, big or small, can be fixed no matter how bad it is. Think about if you tore your favorite shirt. You don't have to throw the shirt away, you fix it by sewing it back together.

Suicide is taking power out of God's hands and putting it into our own hands. If we commit suicide, then what can God do? Nothing. There is so much power in what we do. This can be either positive or negative. We are to give Him everything, including our problems. There's power in surrendering everything to God; there is power in trusting Him.

Scripture:Jeremiah 17:7— 8

Think about the trees: They are on this earth, and they add life and beauty to the earth. Imagine if all the trees were cut down—how would the earth look? Things wouldn't be the same at all. Same with us. We are on this earth to add life and beauty. The Bible says we are the salt of the earth. We are a light that isn't meant to be hidden. We serve a purpose. There are people who need to see *you* personally. No creation is in vain!

Scriptures: Galatians 6:9; Isaiah 40:31;1 Timothy 6:12; Matthew 5:13-16

Can we prevent someone from committing suicide? Possibly. Understand that yes, people have free will; however, as mentioned earlier in chapter 3, we as believers can plant the seed. If you know a person is struggling in this area, pray for them, be a shoulder for them to cry on, listen. Many times, after an individual has died by suicide, family and friends often blame themselves because they feel they could have done more. Even if a person isn't showing any signs of depression or suicidal ideation, still ask The Holy Spirit to show you if they are struggling in this area. He will reveal the answer.

Understand that it's not always about being present for someone physically; many times, it's just sending a person an encouraging text or calling them and giving them an encouraging word. Do as God leads you to do. Sometimes if a person is unable to get out of the house, a visit can be beneficial for them, even if it's a short visit.

Scriptures: Romans 12:15; Philippians 2:1— 8

Every time that I felt suicidal, God always talked me out of it, literally. One time I was alone in my bedroom feeling low, and God had me listen to a song; It wasn't a gospel song, yet the lyrics were about "having a perfect day," "everything going your way," "with nothing standing in your way." God will minister to us in so many different ways, and music is very powerful!

The Lord spoke to me personally and said to me that if I wasn't on this earth, how would He give me dreams and visions and use me to tell family and friends about the stuff that He has shown me?

One time, I was out of town with my older sister, but as I was sleeping, I saw a vision of what suicide would've looked like for me—literally: I saw my dead body lying there, and I felt intense regret and knew that it was a serious thing that I had done. God let me see that this decision wouldn't have given me the results that I had hoped for. I woke up immediately, in shock. But I was glad that I got blocked from performing this action.

I had a dream I was talking to people, and I mentioned not being led by feelings and emotions. These aren't bad per se, but they should not lead us because they are temporary, as they change so much.

What should lead us is God. Our feelings and emotions change constantly; He never changes. Amen!

Scripture: Malachi 3:6

I believe Satan attacked my mind so much because of how creative God made it. Literally, the mind is very powerful. God always gave me very powerful and unique dreams, visions and ideas, early on. The Devil attacked my mind so that he could thwart all the ideas that God put in me from coming to pass. But he failed. Amen!

Therapy greatly helped me with my mental health, as well as some other things. There is nothing wrong with going to therapy. It doesn't make one weak, or crazy. God isn't against therapy at all. He can lead you to the right therapist. Besides being good for mental health, therapy is also good for building confidence, and achieving goals.

CHAPTER SEVEN
POPEYE THE SAILOR MAN

Growing up, one of my favorite cartoons to watch was *Popeye the Sailor Man*. One reason I loved this cartoon so much was that Popeye reminded me of my dad, literally: He was built just like my dad, and he was strong just like my dad—even ate spinach like my dad.

Watching *Popeye the Sailor Man* always made me think of my dad. Not only was my dad strong, he was also hardworking and dedicated. He was fearless like Popeye; he wasn't even scared of anyone who was bigger than him, just like Popeye wasn't scared of Bluto, who was bigger.

Early in my childhood, Dad had a black sundance car, which I thought was really cool. I remember Dad would often take me and my sisters to Blockbuster. I loved Blockbuster; going was a highlight of that time. We would usually go on weekends and rack up on a couple tapes and DVDs, once DVDs became popular.

Now, if you also grew up going to Blockbuster, then you know that you could keep the tapes and DVDs for only a short time, and ultimately, you eventually had to return them, unless you decided to buy them. Well, we used to always keep them for longer periods, and sometimes not even return them at all. Yikes. But we always got grace for this; the Blockbuster workers never gave us any heat about this at all, and funnily enough, up until this very day, I still have a few of the tapes and DVDs that we had failed to return.

Unlike my mom, my dad did grow up in the church, with a Christian family; however, once he reached his adulthood, he kind of got away from the things of God for a bit, as many people do. Now, as a child, I must admit, I did worry about my dad for a few reasons, such as him not seemingly following God like that and him struggling with alcoholism.

It was quite obvious. Of course, The Bible has loads to say about drunkenness.

For a while, my dad seemed quite unfazed. This made me worry greatly about his salvation. I didn't tell him about my worries about his life, instead, I just told my mom about my concerns for him. She would just reassure me and tell me to pray for him, that's it. Things changed a few years later, and he did cut back on the drinking, and he became more serious about the things of God. That made me glad!

Encouragement, Advice, and Reflections

1. Worry about loved ones
2. Is all drinking a sin?
3. All forms of drunkenness
4. Why people get drunk and more
5. If you choose to drink

Maybe you also worry about your loved ones—parents, siblings, friends, etc. Know this: Truly, don't worry or be upset; instead, give all your concerns to God. He can handle everyone and everything. Know this: Just because someone may seem careless of their actions doesn't mean that God isn't dealing with them, and it doesn't mean that the person won't change. Even if the change doesn't come for years, eventually, it will. Understand that a person can indeed be saved, but in a backslidden state.

What does that mean? Well, *backslidden* means a couple things. Basically, it means to slip back into bad habits, sin. If you are truly saved, then that's that. But of course, because we are believers, The Devil will try to tempt us and get us to dabble back in the stuff we used to do, or he will try to entice us with sin, period. But The Bible is clear on how we have the victory and are over-comers. This means that we overcome everything negative that comes our way, including sin. If your loved one is struggling in a specific area, no worries. They will overcome. Amen! The Bible says that God is married to the backslider—meaning He never leaves them no matter what. Literally, "married to" means forever, although in the natural divorces occur. But God doesn't divorce us. He's beyond loyal. Amen! He happily waits for us to return to Him. You may know the story of the prodigal son. If not, please read it. I'll put the scripture below.

Is it a sin to drink at all? Say, light drinking without getting drunk? Now, everyone has different opinions on this. Some, of course, say a believer should not drink at all. All in all, I'll say this: Let God lead you on whether or not to drink at all. If drinking will cause you to stumble, then you probably shouldn't. Me, personally, I drink occasionally. No super-hard liquor, but a glass of wine, champagne, and sometimes a fruity martini cocktail is great. Do I feel any conviction over this? Truthfully, no, and I don't get drunk from any of this.

Does drunkenness apply only to alcohol, though? Well, truthfully, drunkenness can mean a variety of things. Another term for drunkenness could be *glutton*—excess. This means things that we consume in excess. For some people, that can be food that's unhealthy. It could be money for others, spending obsessively; or, for some people, it may even be drugs. Why do people get drunk, over-eat, over-spend and even get high? Well, truthfully, many people do those things as a coping mechanism for difficulties they are facing. But truthfully, only God can truly get you through the trials of life. He doesn't make it where we can just cope. No, He gives us true freedom, victory. Ultimately, only God can truly fill every void in our lives. Imagine eating a big meal and not getting full? When we try to make it through life without God, that's how it feels. God doesn't fills us up temporarily—He fills us up eternally. Amen! Ultimately, the decision to drink is up to the individual. If you choose to drink, have limits, as excessive drinking can lead to health problems.

Scriptures: Jeremiah 3:14; Romans 8:31—39; 1 Corinthians 15:57; Luke15:11—32

Reference

- Hackensack Meridian Health. Binge Drinking: Here's What it Does to Your Body Long Term.

CHAPTER EIGHT
YOUNG AND LOCKED UP

    I have one older brother whom I greatly love, but some things in his life have affected our relationship. He is locked up, literally—not in jail but in prison, and far away. He got locked up when I was just a baby. He would write me constantly when I was a child, though, and I loved this. I would always save all the letters he had written me, and I would be eager to write him. Although he was away, he never missed out on what was happening at home, as I would tell him all in the letters, and I would even send loads of pictures. He saw me go through every age and milestone. I couldn't go visit him physically as a child for a few reasons. Besides the extremely long distance, he was in a maximum security facility which prohibited him from having many visits, and me being under eighteen also meant I couldn't go. I always wished I could go, though I envisioned seeing him in person. To be completely honest, I was a bit oblivious to his situation, I didn't fully understand it and I believed he was coming home any day; he would always mention in his letters how he would be home soon.

    Now, my brother came from my dad's first marriage. My brother's mom, who is now deceased, was a beautiful lady, literally. I loved her so much, and she loved me, my mom, and my sisters as well. There wasn't any bad feelings, whatsoever. My brother was the only child that she had. Now, to be completely honest, my brother's situation never bothered me too much. I had peace despite it because God always spoke to me about it. As I got older, I understood way more, but still, God speaks to me about it, even now.

The first time I went to visit him was at the end of 2011, when I was nineteen years old. He was behind glass, though, due to being in maximum security, but he was still happy to see me and how I had grown up. I remember exactly what I had on that day too. Eventually, things got better though, he ended up getting moved to a correctional facility closer to home and the whole family would visit quite often and he even got more freedom while being there than in the past—he got moved to a lower security level, which allowed him to do more activities and come out of his cell more often. God always makes a way despite the situation. Amen! Now, in chapter 3, I mentioned how after I accepted Jesus, the rest of the family followed. My brother had accepted Jesus while locked up. Amen!

Encouragement, Advice, and Reflections

1. Being locked up
2. Jesus is everywhere
3. Protected
4. Not unforgivable
5. The thief on the cross

Maybe you are someone reading my book who also has a loved in this situation, or maybe you yourself are in this situation currently, or were in this situation in the past. It's no secret that being incarcerated is no joke at all. It can be a difficult, and even scary, situation, but Jesus, ultimately, is everywhere. The Bible is clear that He will never leave nor forsake us no matter what. The whole time that my brother has been locked up, no harm never came his way.

Yeah, he got in a few fights at times, but nothing that damaged him permanently. Some people get killed in prison. Yikes. But God looked out for him, and He will do the same for you or your loved one who is in this situation. God will give an individual in this situation favor as He did with my brother. If you are locked up, currently, I must say this: You have not messed up so bad that God cannot and will not forgive you. Your sin, whatever it is, doesn't disqualify you from God's mercy and forgiveness. You don't have to tell anyone but God what you did. Understand this: Yes, it's nice to receive letters from family, but have you read God's letter? The Bible, which is His Word, that's full of love, encouragement, support, promises, and joy. I encourage you to read that letter! If you desire to accept Jesus, please go back to chapter 3 of my book, and you'll see how to do just that. You don't have to wait to get out to accept Him, and you don't have to be perfect to accept Him. God will give you peace all throughout that facility; He will add light to the darkness. Whether you're in your cell alone or with a roommate, God is there too. You may receive commissary, but ultimately, God has unlimited supply. His son, Jesus, is the ultimate commissary that God gave to the world.

Scriptures:1 John 1:9; Psalm 23; Psalm 37:25; Psalm 69:33; Psalm 94:19; Psalm 146:7; Isaiah 42:7

You may or may not know this, but when Jesus was on the cross, there were two other men beside Him, and one man was a thief. Yet this man repented right before dying, literally. He just cried out to Jesus, and Jesus accepted him. Jesus didn't judge him or turn him away because of his sin, and it wasn't too late. Amen!

Scripture: Luke 23:42–43

CHAPTER NINE
BEWICK

I vividly remember the year 2002 like it was yesterday, me and my family was living in a nice house that I loved; it was big with a spacious living room, with a nice fire place, nice outside and overall just nice everywhere. I loved this house even better than the first house that we lived in, however some changes would soon occur and rather quickly. We ended up having to abruptly move. I remember feeling dissatisfied regarding the move as I had really liked the house that we were in. I was hoping that this move was just a hoax or something, but no it was a reality. I remember the moving van and everything packed and ready to go; however, we didn't move into our new house right away because this move was so abrupt we ended up staying with one of my aunts that summer of 2002. It was cool. It didn't really seem to bother me, and there wasn't much talk about what was going on. Eventually, we left my aunt's house and proceeded to our new house. Now there were just a few problems with the new house. First, the neighborhood was quite rough, which meant riding bikes and playing outside would be limited, or not at all possible. Sigh.

Next, the house had both rats and roaches, which was so gross. I wasn't with this, although I wasn't scared of any bug and insects—and I was not even scared of rodents. I didn't want to live with them. The house had a basement, but it was an unlivable basement, at both of the other houses, it was a livable basement to chill and play in. This basement would also flood quite often, and this basement had a strong odor, so we would often keep the door closed to limit the odor down there. I desperately desired a miracle to happen so that we could move or go back to the other house I liked.

Now we had a cat, and she pretty much caught all the rats, thankfully, but still I didn't desire to live in this house.

Now while living here, things happened, and things were tough, yet God protected us and still made ways. Amen! God is with us wherever we go; the crime rate was definitely very high in this neighborhood. I remember that before we officially moved into the house, I would be embarrassed when people would even ride by and see my family outside. These were people I didn't even know, but still that's how I felt. The house on the outside and the inside did need lots of work done. I remember when we first moved in, the walls were blue and the word b—— was written across the wall in the living room, literally written in big letters. I was appalled. The person who lived there before us had written that on the wall. Eventually, though, the walls got painted white blotting that out, I was glad. Still, I didn't want to be there, but again, God brought peace. But the tough times here was evident. I remember at first that the house didn't even have any carpet or tile on the floors. I didn't like that, but eventually, that got fixed. With the roaches, we stayed stocked up on roach spray.

While living over here, the struggles were real. I remember my dad had a green truck, and one winter, his truck didn't have heat, yet we still needed to get places. The danger was also real while living in this rough neighborhood.

I remember one time, someone did try to get inside the house—a strange man. He kept on coming to the door. God protected us, though. I remember constantly hearing loud, up-close gun-shots while living there. Yikes.

One time, living over here, the house next door to us had caught fire and this happened at night while we were sleeping, fortunately we awoke and got to safety. One of my older cousins just so happened to come over and see us. He said that he felt led. That was The Holy Spirit leading him over. Amen! Had he not shown up and we stayed asleep, the fire could have moved on to our house and killed us. Yikes. God definitely looked out for us.

God has many ways to move, and He will send help. Amen! This proves God is more powerful than any danger whatsoever, and He can use whoever to save you. The house next door burning down ultimately was a blessing because it was a drug and prostitution house. Yikes.

Another time, I remember that while living over there, someone did try to get in my dad's truck. They had picked at the lock a bit, which in turn messed up the door a bit, like jammed it, making it hard to open. God definitely protected us while we were over there. The Bible says no weapon formed against us shall prosper; nothing deadly shall harm us. Amen!

As I got older, I was embarrassed to invite any friends over, or even to let people know where I lived at all! When people would ask, I would make an excuse for why they couldn't come over.

God kept speaking to me about my family moving from over there, though.

Literally, He would speak about it over and over, and I would have recurring dreams about it. God isn't oblivious to our situations, and He won't leave us in the wilderness. Amen!

The longer we lived over here, the more things continued to get worse—more danger and more rats and roaches.

Yikes. I remember one night being in the kitchen and roaches all just coming from behind the refrigerator, and even coming out of the walls, literally. I was spraying non-stop, and they just kept coming. I feel I had gotten numb to this situation—meaning I was in denial of how bad the situation was, and in many ways, I just zoned out. But obviously, it was a bother to me. Now we ended up moving out of this house twelve years later, and honestly, I had to get used to living better because I had gotten so programmed living in that situation that it became normal. Unfortunately, many times we become used to things that aren't good for us. I must admit once we moved into the new house, I still had some struggles, because I was now basically even older and finally fully processing the whole situation. It was mind-blowing to have experienced all of that for so long, and now to be seeing something different.

Encouragement, Advice, and Reflections

1. The lion's den
2. The little things
3. In the world but not of it
4. Used to

You may know the story of Daniel in the lion's den. If you don't, or aren't a believer yet and don't know, long story short, Daniel was a man in The Bible, and he was in a dangerous situation—in a den full of lions, However, while he was in this den, the lions didn't harm him at all. They stayed still. Amen! God will keep harm away from us while we are in the den, whether it's our living situation, our job, etc. He will keep all the lions in our lives still. While we were in that dangerous living situation, God kept the thieves, shooters, and murderers still. They did us no harm Amen! You can find this story in Daniel 6.

While we were living over there. My cat used to always run away from home. She would randomly get out and be gone for weeks at a time in that very rough neighborhood. Yikes. I'd be worried that she had died or gotten attacked, but no, she would always return home safe, in one piece. Amen! God cares about the very little thing. He will perfect that which concerns us. He protected our whole family, including the cat. He is great! With Him, there are no limits, and no one is left out. Amen! He cares about His whole creation. Don't take God's protection for granted. The Bible mentions how we are in the world, but not of it, and this is true. There's so much danger on the earth, yet God keeps us protected daily. Praise God every day that you wake up, and go out in the dangerous world, and return home in one piece.

The reality is that many people are used to living this kind of way. Unfortunately, for some people, living in a bad home and neighborhood is the norm. That's how it was for them and their whole family, including their grandparents, parents, etc, but this is neither normal nor the will of God. Unfortunately, there are some churches that believe that if you're a believer, God basically wants you living this way. Understand that prosperity isn't a sin. It's God's will. He wants His children living at their best. Prosperity isn't just limited to one area—it includes everything being well. Don't settle for what you know. Break those generational curses of struggle living. Many people have succeeded in breaking the generational curse of poverty and were the very first millionaires in their entire family. Amen! With God, all things are possible.

As mentioned earlier in my book, in the '70s sitcom *Good Times*, the characters lived in poverty for years, but on the very last episode, they finally made it out. God wants to bring you out. Don't limit yourself to what you're used to, and don't limit where God can take you based on your circumstances. Poverty can't stop your purpose!

Scriptures: Deuteronomy 31:6; Psalm 23; Psalm 37:25; Isaiah 59:19; Hebrews 12:29

CHAPTER TEN
YOUNG AND PAID

I remember when I got my very first job, I was ecstatic. Though it was just a janitor's job and it didn't pay much, I was still glad because I desired to work. I always wanted to be "independent" by all means. I first worked morning shift though I wasn't a morning person I managed and getting off early was good.

Eventually, I had switched to the evening shift, which was still pretty good, but tiring. At first, we got off at 11:30 p.m. Then things changed to 1:30 a.m. Yet I managed, but I must admit getting off at that time was exhausting.

This job was pretty easy, though, obviously. But I must admit—working at this job was a very impromptu decision for me. I didn't really think this through.

I made this decision based on my emotions, as this was something I *needed*. I didn't even consult with God whether this was the job for me or the place to work. We all can do this. Many times, our decisions are based on our own needs. Over time working here became a bit draining. Now, I'm not saying working here was draining because of the job itself; rather it was because I wasn't where God was leading me. It's important to go only where God sends you. If God puts you somewhere, you will know, and there will be confirmation from The Holy Spirit, as well as that peace.

Scripture: Proverbs 19:21

As time went on, things weren't progressing here for me at all, and many problems began to ensue. Now I found myself becoming more and more tired of being here. I began looking for other jobs, and even desired to find my true purpose, though I had no clue at all. Sighs. I was only working this job part time. I never got to full-time, though there was mention of that.

Truthfully, I was working here because I didn't trust God regarding my purpose, and I wasn't ready to fully submit to His plans for my life. After I finished all my work, I would often sit alone and away from everyone just to recoup. Many people encouraged me to leave, stating that I was young and shouldn't limit myself, which I agreed with wholeheartedly. I ended up making it a year and almost two months working here. I was fired after that, and this firing came abruptly, no questions asked. I was in a way relived because I wanted a new beginning, but at the same time, I was thinking, what was I going to do next?

Well, I can testify that God was faithful and took care of me. I never missed out on anything I needed at all.

Now, I did work another job about a year later, and that job lasted me only a few weeks. Yikes.

However, I walked away with a check. God is so good. Amen! The best Father to exist. Take His advice, that's in his Word! He's got you and won't drop you. There's nothing wrong with independence, but no one is ever so independent that they don't need someone to cover their back at all. This doesn't make one weak! We can all fall down at some point, as this life comes with many hidden curveballs. God often removes the dead-end things so that He can bring what's new, better. Sometimes things can be harmful to us without us even realizing it, like staying somewhere where God didn't put you. I think about what would have happened had I stayed at the janitor job. If I wouldn't gotten fired, I wouldn't have grown in my faith and learned to trust God completely for all my needs, I probably wouldn't have written my book. I would just have been stuck there for years doing the same ole thing day-by-day. Some removals are divine. Amen!

Know when it's time to go. It takes faith to let go as well. Sometimes we should say,

Lord, remove me from this job, this place, this person, etc. Even with me writing my book, to be completely honest, I didn't have the funds to put this book together. I simply had faith. God made a way for it all to come together. Amen!

God doesn't look at our financial situation when He calls us to do things.

He wants us to simply trust Him.

You're not unqualified to do what He has called you to do. He will always make a way out of no way. Many times, we say, "I'll do it when I have the money," "when I'm in a better position, etc. But no, do it now! God will provide what's needed.

Don't disqualify yourself from the dreams that God put in you due to something as simple as finances. In the natural, provision is limited; in the spiritual, it's unlimited! Lastly, I'll leave you with this:

"Being a believer without faith is like being a child without imagination."

Scriptures: Psalm 20:7;Psalm 37:5; Psalm 121;Matthew 6:25—34; Mark 4:19; Romans 8:28; Isaiah 49:15; Philippians 4:11—13

Encouragement, Advice, and Reflections

1. Your job matters
2. God provides
3. Money the truth
4. Jesus feeding the 5000
5. Impressive people

Now, I am not saying there's anything wrong with being a janitor. If this is you, don't down yourself because of your position. *Everything* is valuable to God. Amen! It's not where you start—it's where you finish. Don't limit where God can use you, and do your absolute best!
  Scriptures: Zechariah 4:10; Colossians 3:23—24; Matthew 7:11

Ultimately, don't put your trust in a job even if it's a top-notch title that pays well. God is our provider—even the best job can fail us, but He cannot. Amen! There are so many people in The Bible that God provided for. If He did it for them, He will do it for you. It takes faith to believe this, but it's true. Ask yourself this question: If You lost your job tomorrow, would you be in panic mode, or would you have trust Him above to carry you through as promised?

Jesus's needs were met while he was on this earth. You may know the story of when He fed the five thousand though He had only five loaves of bread and two fish.

For years I sought validation through a job, a career. I thought finding the perfect job and career would make me happy and ultimately make me somebody. There's nothing wrong with either of those things, nothing wrong about money, although some churches that I encountered taught that it was. God isn't against us having or even desiring money at all. However, we shouldn't make it an idol or use it for evil, or even just for personal purposes—not that we can't give ourselves nice things. But if God blesses us, it's for a higher purpose, and that's so we can bless others and expand His kingdom. Ultimately, money can't buy happiness. I remember hearing this all the time as a child, and I didn't quite understand, but now I do. When it comes to the desire for money, always check your motives. True lasting happiness comes from God alone!

Scriptures: Proverbs 11:25; Deuteronomy 28:12; Matthew 14:13—21

We often look at people and are impressed by what they have—their house, their car, their position, etc. Who's someone with wealth that you admire? Ultimately, these things impress us, but we cannot impress God by these things. There is truly only one thing that impresses God. Please go back to the beginning of my book, in my preface, and you'll find out what that one thing is. Ultimately, remember: only what you do for Christ will last!

Scriptures: Mark 8:36; 1 Corinthians 4:7—9; Psalm 37:25

CHAPTER ELEVEN
YOUNG AND TAKEN

Part 1

Warning: viewer discretion advised. The topics discussed in this chapter contain explicit details and words. This chapter is not to offend or scare anyone, but it's a topic that needs to be discussed. I advise you, if topics regarding sex will trigger you in any way, to please skip reading. If you are a parent reading this chapter, please, I urge you to discuss the topics mentioned in this chapter with your children. Don't wait. If you are a teen or a young adult, I advise you to read this chapter with your parents or someone that you love and trust and can talk to without judgment. But overall, have no fear about this chapter because it is important. But please, let God lead you. Thanks!

I must ask you, the reader this question: Have you ever had a sexual act done to your body without your control?

Think long and hard. Did something happen early in your childhood, teen years, or early adulthood? Or even in your middle or late adulthood? Do you remember how it made you feel? If anything was done to your body that was out of your control, or if anything was done that made you uncomfortable, that was rape. Another term for rape is *sexual abuse* or *sexual assault*; and depending on your age, if you're a minor under eighteen, it's called *molestation* or *statutory rape*.

    Let's dive into what exactly rape is: It's a sexual activity that is unwanted, but is forced, pressured, or manipulated upon the victim. Rape is a serious crime. This book chapter will be using direct terms when it comes to body parts. It's important to understand and know exactly what parts of your body are called and what exactly those body parts do and are for so that if you were to find yourself in this situation, you would know how to properly communicate with your parents and the police. You'd be able to effectively distinguish exactly in what part of your body you were touched. Some people refer to certain body parts as genitals, which is fine, but there's more in-depth terms. If you are a female reading, know that you have breasts, nipples, hips, thighs, navel, a butt and butt hole, which is known as the anus, a vagina, vulva, clitoris, perineum, and urethra which is the hole that you urinate from; your vagina has a separate hole. I advise you to look up the female anatomy to know exactly where everything is located and how exactly everything functions. Now the vaginal hole is where a male's penis goes in for penetration. To penetrate means to insert or slip something into. If you have gone through puberty, which is typically between ages nine through twelve, then you more than likely have hair covering your vaginal area, better known as pubic hair. The pubic hair covers all of the outward part of the vagina, and there can also be pubic hair in between your thighs.

    After penetration, the penis is then used to sexually pleasure a woman; usually, this is done by the penis being moved in and out, back and forth. The penis also releases fluids known as semen during sex. This is known as ejaculation, semen contains sperm which is what causes a pregnancy to occur. I also advise you to look up the male anatomy to know exactly where everything is and exactly how everything functions. A male can sexually pleasure a female's vagina in many ways. Besides penetrating the vagina for sexual pleasure, a male can also use his mouth and tongue on a female's vagina and body. This is called oral sex. It's done by licking and sucking. A man can also use his fingers, or even sex toys, to pleasure the vagina. Penetration can occur in the anus as well—this is called anal sex.

Vaginal penetration can occur from different angles, frontward, backward, or sideways. However, there must be consent for any of this. Has a male ever penetrated your vagina from any of the mentioned angles without your permission? Or penetrated your anus or touched, or even licked your perineum?

A male your age or older? If so, you were raped. If you are under eighteen and it was an older male, it was statutory rape.

Statutory rape is wrong; a minor cannot give consent at all. Please, if you are a child who has been a victim of statutory rape, molestation, it's not your fault at all. Don't be afraid, and don't be silent. I urge you to tell your parents or a trusted adult who you know will support you. However, let me clarify this: Children can rape other children, and teens can rape other teens. Even if you're in a committed relationship with a guy, he can rape you.

A couple things to note about rape: It can be done to different degrees, but it doesn't matter to what degree it's done, and it doesn't matter if it's done for a short minute or for hours—it's still very serious. If you are a female and a male just rubs his penis on your vagina, anus, vulva, clitoris, perineum—whether it be the inner or outer parts without your consent—it's rape. If a male sticks only his fingers, whether it's just one finger or all ten fingers inside or outside your vaginal or anal area without your consent, it's rape. Even if a male just simply touches or rubs your pubic hair or if he makes you touch his pubic hair without your consent, it's rape. If a male just touches your vagina without your consent while you are fully clothed or partially clothed, it's rape. If you are fully clothed and a male humps you without permission, it's rape. Humping while wearing clothes is known as dry humping. Another example of rape while fully clothed would be if a male pulls up your shirt only and sucks your nipples, or if they only pull up your dress or skirt or pull down your pants to penetrate you.

An example of rape while partially clothed would be if you're in your bra and panties and a male was to pull your nipples out of your bra without your consent and suck on them, or if he just put his hands in your bra and squeezed our breasts, and if he moved your panties to the side and penetrated you that way.

If a male licks, sucks, or nibbles on your vagina, breasts, nipples, navel, butt, anus, perineum, stomach, or neck without your consent, it's rape. If he uses any toys, oils, lubricants, etc, on or in any part of your body, without your consent, it's rape. A male kissing you without your permission is rape; whether it's your lips, cheek, inner thighs, neck, stomach, back, breast, nipples, navel, etc. If a male just makes you play with his penis with your hands; fingers without consent it's rape. If a male just touches, slaps or grabs you on the butt without permission with rape; if a male just squeezes on your breast, nipples, clitoris without your consent it's rape. If he ejaculates; releases sperm; semen; fluids on your breast, nipples, clitoris, butt, stomach, back, legs, hips, thighs, urethra, clitoris, vagina; inside or out, vulva, navel, face, eyes, lashes, brows, head; including the hair on your head; real or faux without your permission this is rape; even if a male goes far as peeing on you without permission this is rape; or if he makes you pee on him. If a male rubs, licks or touches you on or near your hips or thighs without permission it's rape. If a male simply puts his fingers in or on your urethra or rubs his penis on or near it without consent it's rape. If a male chokes you or uses handcuffs on you during sex and you don't consent to that it's rape. If a male has sex with you while you're menstruating and you don't consent to that it's rape. Women can rape other women; if a woman performs any sex acts on you that you don't consent to it's rape; even if she uses a fake penis; dildo, even if you are a lesbian; transgender female still no one has the right to touch your body without your permission or make you do things that you're uncomfortable with. Consent must always be given to everything, if you agree to let a male do oral sex on you, but you don't want him to penetrate you and he does it anyway this is rape; consent should always be given before moving on to different sexual acts; agreeing to one thing doesn't mean agreeing to another thing unless, clearly stated and you always have the right to say no! If a male makes you perform oral sex; putting his penis in your mouth; even if he just makes you lick it without fully inserting it into his mouth it's rape, if you agree to perform oral sex on a male, but he ejaculates inside of your mouth without your consent it's rape, even if a male makes you have sex in a position that you're uncomfortable with; in or makes you have sex somewhere you're uncomfortable at such as in public; outdoors, car or on the floor this is rape. If a male films you without your consent it's abuse. Sex should never be forced, pressured, bribed or manipulated.

With speaking up understand this: speaking up can mean many different things, I understand some people may not want to speak up at all or some people may not want to speak up right away.

Speak up when you feel comfortable ultimately; even if you don't never tell it to the police, tell someone you are comfortable with; family who's supportive, close friends, a therapist etc. don't suppress it completely. God ultimately will deal with the individual who harmed you; God is just! Amen!

Since you've heard the word consent. what exactly does it mean? Well firstly as mentioned above the word "control" which means to be in charge of; we are all in charge of our own bodies, no one else's. Consent also means "willingness" which means the quality or state of being prepared to do something; readiness.

Synonyms of willingness are desire, inclination, eagerness, enthusiasm, will, wish, keenness. Antonyms of willingness are reluctance, and unwillingness.

Consent is also permission for something to happen or agreement to do something. To consent to something you must have full understanding beforehand and be in the right state of mind as well.

In easier terms consent means actively and verbally saying yes and also saying yes with enthusiasm, not just shaking your head or not even saying yes via text or phone, but saying yes in person. To clarify always look for yes instead of yeah or ok, because yeah or ok isn't as secure as yes. yeah or okay can just mean I'm doing so because I feel I have to or I'm unsure still. Only after the active verbal clear yes, then look for the individual showing yes through their body language as well meaning comfortable relaxed, not tense or showing any signs of nervousness or anxiety, and also willingness and consent starts in the heart. If you have sex and you know in your heart that you don't really want to or don't feel truly ready, then that's not true consent, always pay attention to how you feel and don't ignore how you feel.

Reference
- RAINN. #ConsentRULES
- The University of Sydney What enthusiastic consent actually looks like:If it's not an enthusiastic yes, it's a no.

Encouragement, Advice, and Reflections

1. Blaming and Shaming
2. Respect Women
3. Real Men
4. The purity movement
5. Pregnancy in the church
6. Lust the truth
7. Slut shaming

One thing I have noticed that really bothers me, especially in a church setting, is how often the women are blamed for the men's struggles with lust and are often told not to show too much of their bodies to avoid tempting the men. Even just in society, in general, women are often told that men are completely sexual beings who have limited self-control, and that men highly crave sex; therefore, if a woman wears anything sexy that shows off her body, she is basically setting herself up to get raped, and it's her fault if a man rapes her or cat-calls her while she's in a sexy outfit. Please, never tell a young girl or woman this very ignorant statement. I highly disagree with this and get tired of hearing it. These types of comments normalize rape.

Firstly, women should be able to wear absolutely whatever they feel confident enough to wear. No one should be disrespected due to their clothing. Even if a woman is a stripper, she doesn't deserve to be violated—and no, I'm not saying go get a job as a stripper—I'm just being completely honest.

The world should respect women! Truthfully, and contrary to popular belief, clothing, or lack of, has no bearing on rape, Predators often go for vulnerability, understand that. But this is still no excuse. Vulnerability can mean a variety of things—but usually, its manifested by someone who may not have much knowledge, someone perceived as naïve, someone who is deemed as weaker because of their young age, a quiet demeanor, disabilities, or low self-esteem, someone who wants and needs love. Rape isn't even about sex—it's actually about power and control. Many people try to gain their power by taking others.'

Ladies reading my book, keep on being sexy and let no one tell you otherwise. Your body is beautiful—embrace it. I hate how often young girls, particularly black girls, are told that they're fast" or "too grown." This is a ridiculous statement, and this qualifies as sexualizing a child. Understand a child is just that—a child. Wearing make-up, certain hairstyles, or certain clothes does not equate to being fast or too grown, and a young girl's developing body isn't bad either. It's's all normal. An adult should not look at or comment on a child's appearance in this type of way, never. Even when a young girl gets pregnant, she is judged, referred to as "fast," but the reality is that many times, when a girl is pregnant at a very young age, it is often the result of rape, or even incest. No one should judge, if a girl is pregnant from either of those situations yet, she made the courageous decision to proceed with the pregnancy. I think that's amazing and shows a great deal of strength.

For years, women's bodies have been policed. Enough is enough! A real man will respect a woman, period. A real man has self-control. If you are a man reading my book who respects women, I love and appreciate you. Keep on. Set the example for all others. Let's stop holding victims accountable for rape and hold the perpetrators accountable instead.

Scriptures; Proverbs 27:5; Proverbs 28:13; Galatians 5:23

Reference

- Ceasar, Chanda The Sexualization of Children and How This Can Impact Your Child Sexual Abuse Survivor: 4 Tips to Help Them Stop Blaming Themselves for the Sexual Abuse They Endured

- Douglas, Teresa 8 Things NOT to Say to Your DaughterGirls shouldn't ever have to hear these words. August 10, 2024
- Glaser, Josh Is A Woman Responsible for a Man's Lust Regeneration 11 minute read.
- Martin, Melanie Let's Stop Oversexualizing Black Girls and Women. Ebony. June 6, 2022.
- Rape Crisis England and Wales.Myths vs Facts: Helping You Heal from Trauma.
- Seven, Zuva What Is Toxic Femininity? Reviewed by Ivy Kwong LMFT, VerywellMind. UC Santa Cruz.Center For Advocacy, Resources &
- Empowerment (Care). Common
- Misconceptions about Sexual Violence.

Throughout my life, I have been to many churches that seemed to have an obsession with virginity. In some churches, virginity is often marked as a high, noble prize, and even, in some cases, a part of salvation. Now, there is nothing wrong with being a virgin; however, my issue is that the purity movement often shames those who are not virgins without understanding that there are many individuals who were raped, which is why they lost their virginity. Many individuals, after a rape, do feel that their self-worth is diminished, so the church should be careful of stuff like this. I remember as a teen at a church I attended that there was a sermon session about sex for the youth, but, there wasn't much talk about rape or incest that I recall—just mainly talk about fornication, which means sex with someone you're not married to. There was also talk about masturbation and not getting pregnant young and unmarried.

Getting married many times in church settings is sometimes deemed as a method to avoid sexual sin, as if basically, if you get married, it'll fix those issues instantly, but no, that's not the case. You can be married and still struggle with sexual sin, such as infidelity and many more. With pregnancy, I feel the church can be very biased, and for these reasons, many times, young girls and women avoid coming to church, or leave their church altogether for fear of judgement. In many cases, the church's judgement on pregnancy may even lead a young girl or woman to secretly get an abortion. I've heard many women admit to doing this because they wanted to avoid being shamed and talked badly about by the church.

Now, I do remember specifically in the youth sessions on sex that the youth leader had said that if a girl gets pregnant, she has to leave and can no longer be a part of the youth church. Why are young girls and women always punished for pregnancy? They don't impregnate themselves; nothing is ever said to the guys who impregnate them. Pregnancy itself is not a sin. Every living thing on this earth all came from a pregnancy—animals, bugs, insects, even Jesus himself, came from a pregnancy, so believing that pregnancy is a sin is contradictory.

I've heard some churches bring up pregnancy basically in a generational-curse type of sense, like if a mother, daughter, and granddaughter all repeatedly became pregnant. I must say this: a baby is not a curse or a punishment. Let's remember, God is the creator. He is the one who creates people and children, and He certainly doesn't curse people. Fear and shame should not be used as methods to stop teenage and out of wedlock pregnancy. For me myself, growing up hearing those types of statements put fear into me about becoming pregnant. I too feared how I would be judged by the church if I ever got into that situation. Ultimately, the church should be a place that represents God's love, support, and forgiveness! Many times, the church can seem hypocritical to many individuals, which makes them stay distant. We can't preach about love and forgiveness and not show it to others! Hence the expression "practice what you preach."

Scriptures: John 8:7; John 13:35; 1 John 3:18

Reference
- Cole, Cameron Critique Purity Culture, but Teach Sexual Ethics to Teens The Gospel Coalition September 21, 2021.
- Ford, Amy Unplanned Pregnancies: How Should The Church Respond? Focus on the Family April 29, 2022.

If any man or woman is struggling with lust, that's a personal issue that one must work through themselves. No one can truly make you lust after them—that's a choice you make. I feel that often times, in the church, attraction, in general, is often seen as a bad thing. Physical attraction to someone isn't bad or sinful. It's a natural part of being a human for both men and women. There's a difference between being attracted to someone and lusting after someone.

Women are often referred to as being slutty or whorish for talking about sex or liking sex at all. In many church settings, I've heard how a woman is supposed to have sex only to please her husband and to produce children. However, a woman talking about, liking, or enjoying sex does not make her a slut or a whore. Her role, sexually, isn't solely to please her husband and reproduce. Both men and women were created with sexual hormones and desires. This is natural! Sexual pleasure is not only for men. I feel that slut shaming is also another reason why young girls and women don't speak up about sexual abuse; instead they blame themselves for it.

Reference
- Planned Parenthood. What is slut shaming? by Miriam@planned parenthood June 9, 2023 4-minute read

Part 2

If you are reading this chapter of my book and you are male, know that you have a penis. Your penis has a head, the tip at the end. Your penis has a sac attached to it, the scrotum.

You have a perineum, a urethra, which is the hole you urinate from, you have a chest, nipples, a stomach, a navel, a butt, a butt hole, anus, hips, and thighs; and if you've gone through puberty, then you too probably have pubic hair surrounding your penis. You also have hair on your chest if you're in that age range. I advise you to look up the male anatomy to know exactly where everything is located and exactly how everything functions. I also advise you to look up the female anatomy to know where everything is located and what everything does.

Now when it comes to the hole that you urinate from, this same hole is also for ejaculating, releasing semen and sperm which, are released during sex.

Your penis is used to penetrate a female's vagina. To penetrate means to insert your penis, which is also used to pleasure her, which is done by moving it in and out, back and forth. A female can do many things with a man's penis to pleasure him: she can ride on top of a man's penis from many different angles—frontwards, backwards, sideways. She can lick and suck on a man's penis to pleasure him. This is known as oral sex. Or she simply can pleasure a man by rubbing and playing with his penis with her hands and fingers.

However, consent must be given for any of this. If a female makes you penetrate her vagina from any angle—frontwards, sideways, or backwards—without your consent, it's rape. If she makes you lick, suck, or nibble on any part of her vagina, breasts, nipples, stomach, anus, navel, or perineum without your consent, it's rape.

If she makes you insert your penis in her anus without your consent, it's rape.

If a female touches your penis—any part of it, even just half of it, the tip only, or all of it, including the scrotum, it's rape if you don't consent for her to touch it. If she even just touches the area you pee, ejaculate from, it's rape if you don't consent. If she fingers you, whether with one finger or all ten, in your anus or perineum area without your permission, it's rape. If a female chokes you or uses handcuffs on you without your consent, it's rape. If a female makes you have sex with her while she's menstruating and you don't consent to that, it's rape. If a female licks, sucks, or nibbles on any part of your chest, stomach, nipples, butt, anus, perineum, or navel without permission, it's rape.

Rape can occur whether you're fully or partially clothed, whether she just dry-humps on you or make you dry-hump her. Another example of rape fully clothed would be if a female just makes you pull your penis out of your pants to perform oral sex on you or to ride your penis or to make you penetrate her or if she just makes you open and unbutton or pull up your shirt to lick or suck on you.

An example of rape while partially clothed would be if you're just in your boxers, underwear and she makes you pull your penis out of them or puts her hands in your boxers, underwear or if you're in your bath-robe and she makes you open the robe, or if she just goes underneath your robe from any angle. If a female just rubs her vagina on your penis or mouth and you don't consent, it's rape. If you agree to perform oral sex on a female, but then she makes you penetrate her without your consent, it's rape. If a male is a minor, he cannot consent to sex, and it's still molestation, statutory rape.

If a female kisses you without permission anywhere, it's rape, whether it's your lips, cheek, neck, navel, stomach, inner thighs, penis, chest, nipples, or back. If a female touches, rubs, or licks you on or near your hips and thighs without permission, it's rape.

If a female just simply touches or rubs your pubic hair without your consent, it's rape. Or if she makes you just touch her pubic hair, if she just rubs or touches the hair on your chest without your consent, it's rape. If a female makes you ejaculate inside her mouth or anywhere on her body—stomach, vagina, inside or outside, vulva, breasts, nipples, face, head, including the hair on her head real or faux, eyes, lashes, brows, butt, back, leg, thighs, or navel without your consent, it's rape.

Women can release fluids during sex as well. If a woman releases any fluid from her vagina onto any part of your body without your consent, it's also rape.

Men can rape other men as well. If a man performs any sex acts on you that you don't consent to, it's rape, even if you are a gay, transgender male—no one has the right to touch your body without your permission or make you do things that you're uncomfortable with.

It's a big misconception that straight males can't be raped and that only gay and transgender men get raped. Now, if you are a straight male who was raped, it doesn't make you weak or less manly.

You are still human. Even if you're in a committed relationship with a female and she does anything listed above without your permission, it's still rape. If a female just makes you lay your penis on the outward part of her vagina without consent, it's rape. It's also rape if a female manipulates you to ejaculate, such as by playing with your penis, rubbing or squeezing it. If a female makes you pee on her or if she pees on you without consent, it's rape. If she makes you have sex in a position that you're comfortable with or makes you have sex in a place that your uncomfortable with, such as in public, outdoors, on the floor, in a car, etc, it's rape.

If a female films you without your consent, it's abuse. If a female uses any toys or oils and lubricants on or in any part of your body, without your consent, it's rape. It's a misconception that women can't rape men and a misconception that only men pressure women for sex; many times, women pressure men for sex, or pressure them to go further than they would like. Contrary to popular belief that males are always in the mood for sex, they can have fears regarding sex. Males of any age can have sexual issues, like erectile dysfunction.

This can affect their ability to get aroused to have sex, especially if a man or boy has been abused sexually, which may contribute to those types of issues.

Reference
- Fredonia, State University Of New York. Male Survivors.
- WashU. Masculine Identified Survivors: Myths about Sexual and Relationship Violence Against Masculine Identified People.
- Foss, Kevin What is Toxic Masculinity and How it Impacts Mental Health Anxiety and Depression Association of America. November 14, 2022

Part 3

When it comes to sex, it is important to communicate about preferences regarding protection, better known as contraception. There are many different forms of contraception, but mainly condoms and birth control. A male uses a condom over his penis to prevent pregnancy and STDs, and a female uses birth control to prevent pregnancy, but, birth control doesn't protect against STDs, which is why the male uses a condom. If a person has sex with you without using any contraception and you don't consent to that, it's rape. If a male ejaculates inside of a female's vagina, even if she is on birth control or can't bear children naturally, it's still rape if she doesn't give consent to that. If you're having sex and the condom breaks, rips, slits, tears, or slips off, both parties should stop immediately and ask how each would like to proceed. If you want to completely stop, the other party should respect that. If you're okay with proceeding with out the condom, then give consent to that. Otherwise, a completely new condom should be put on. If anyone sneaks the condom off or puts holes in it without the other party's knowledge or consent, that's rape and manipulation.

If you're a male and a female forces or pressures you to have sex with her without a condom, or if she forces or pressures you to ejaculates inside her vagina without your consent, but she lies to you about being on birth control or fakes taking her birth control by putting the pill in her mouth and hiding it under her tongue this is rape, and also a form of manipulation. Even if it's your spouse, contraception should be used unless both party's agree otherwise. Even if a person uses contraceptives fully and correctly how they are supposed to be used, that still doesn't mean they can't rape you or make it okay for them to rape you. Even if there is agreement to unprotected sex, but either party requests the pull-out method, yet there is manipulation of not pulling out, this is rape.

Reference
- Rape Crisis England & Wales.What Is Stealthing.
- Sexual Violence Prevention.Pregnancy Resulting from Sexual Violence.

Encouragement, Advice, and Reflections

1. Big question
2. God's goodness
3. Equal

Is abortion ever reasonable in the case of a pregnancy from rape or incest? Well, let's understand a few things: All life is precious to God. As mentioned earlier, pregnancy is not a sin however it comes about. Understand that God is good in every situation—even in the worst situations. He is not just good, He is also faithful. Even in the worst situation, God can use it for his glory. He can turn a mess into a masterpiece. Many of us were born from non-ideal circumstances, yet God used us for His glory, and He doesn't look at us from the circumstances that we came from. Remember, God is no respecter of persons—meaning: He views everyone as equal no matter what. Jesus's death was to save all lives!

Scriptures: 1 Thessalonians 5:18; Romans 2:11; Psalm 139:14; Mark 10:45

Part 4

If a person has sex but isn't able to properly consent due to intoxication on drugs or alcohol, it's rape. If a person is manipulated into sex by drugs or alcohol, it's rape. If a person is passed out drunk and an individual has sex with them while they are in that state, it's rape.

Clear, full verbal consent must be given in this case prior to the acts—consent to have sex and consent to drinks, etc. If a person exhibits slurred speech or blurry vision due to being under the influence, they can't consent. If both parties consent to the use of any drugs or alcohol during sex, there should be a limit on how much each will consume, and both parties should not exceed that limit. If either one person or both parties show signs of extreme drunkenness or extreme signs of being drugged sex should be completely avoided. Why? Because when a person is under the influence of drugs or alcohol, they can't properly make decisions. If you're extremely drunk or high, you may agree to stuff that you normally wouldn't agree to. Even if you were drunk or drugged and got raped, you are still not at fault. Being drunk or high gives no one any right to take advantage of you! Even if it's just a simple over-the-counter drug that is used, as many over-the-counter drugs can cause drowsiness and changes to the brain and even to the vision.

Reference
- RAINN.Drug-Facilitated Sexual Assault.

Part 5

When an individual has any physical or verbal disabilities that will impact consent, such as being handicapped, (in a wheel chair)—any missing limbs, deaf, blind, mute, weakened muscles, not being in the right mind or mental state, severe mental illness, etc. These could all greatly impact an individual's ability to properly give consent. If a person has sex with someone who is unable to give proper consent due to any of these issues, it's rape. A person with disabilities can give consent; however, it would be necessary for them to discuss their disabilities beforehand for the best comfortable experience and their boundaries should be respected based on their disabilities. If a person is deaf, they would need hearing aids to properly hear and communicate and consent if a person is mute, they would need to use writing, sign language, as well as body language to consent. Otherwise, if someone just has sex with them, ignoring their disabilities, it would be rape.

Scripture: Proverbs 31:8– 9

Reference
- Hood, Chelsea Sexual Violence Against People with Disabilities, Maryland Coalition Against Sexual Assault.July 13, 2022.

Part 6

I remember when I was fifteen, my family was at a water park, and I remember I was alone for a few minutes, I was actually walking to the other side to get back to my family when this old man spoke to me in a flirty way. He said, How are you doing? Literally in a voice that was trying to make me feel comfortable. I didn't even speak. I immediately ignored him and got away.

What is a predator, exactly? Predators are very manipulative individuals, which is why it's hard many times to recognize them because most predators aren't big, mean, or scary.

They look like average, everyday, normal people; and many times, they be can be very kind and loving. Predators often manipulate victims with attention, love, gifts, and money. Please know this:

A person can give you gifts and nice things and still be no good, even evil. This is why discernment is important.

Predators are very keen, smart, and precise at what they do and how they do it, unfortunately, which is also why, often times, they don't get caught. Anyone can be a predator—a parent, grandparent, a teacher, a pastor, a daycare provider, a doctor, a nurse, an aunt or uncle, etc. Know the signs! Children, teens, and adults can be preyed upon.

You've heard me mention the word *incest*. If you don't know what it is, it's sexual abuse that occurs within families.

Say, if a father has sex with his daughter, if a mother has sex with her son, or if two cousins have sex or if two siblings have sex with each other.

Understand that this is not okay. The Devil likes to distort families and likes to distort what God truly intended sex to be.

God is not the author of confusion. If you have had a sexual relationship with your family member, whoever it is, please understand this is abusive, toxic. I pray that God makes a way of escape for you!

Reference
- RAINN, Incest.

Encouragement, Advice, and Reflections

1. Predators in the Church
2. Discernment

Church is the last place that you'd expect to find a predator, right? Well, unfortunately, there are many predators in the church, both women and men. Not every person in church is right or there for the right reasons. The Bible talks about wolves in sheep's clothing—people who portray to be godly, but really aren't. Deception is very real. Even if someone in church is in the pulpit, it doesn't t mean that they are right or ultimately from God! The Bible also says tests the spirits, to see if they are truly from God. Pray for Him to open your eyes thoroughly.

Scriptures: 1 John 4:1; 2 Peter 2:1—22; Matthew 7:15, Matthew 15:14; Matthew 24:11; 2 Thessalonians 2:1—3; 1 Timothy 4:1—5

Reference
- Rainer, Sam. Predators, Wolves, and Recognizing Where Abuse Begins in Churches.
- President and senior consultant

When I was thirteen years old, I remember I was at church one night. I had on a cute outfit. Now, I remember exactly what I had on—it was some jeans and a brown cami top with what at the time was called a "srug" over it. The srug was dark brown with some specks of gold glitter on it. I remember this man at the church had commented on my outfit, and he said to me, "No more cleavage."

Now at thirteen years old, I didn't even know what cleavage was, and if you also don't know what it is, cleavage is the noticeable hollow between a girl or woman's breasts. A grown man had absolutely no business looking at my body, period. It doesn't matter how shapely built a child or teen's body is, a man or woman has no right to comment, period. I remember the man at church even called me "sweetie" "a big red flag." Predators often give children nicknames to make the child feel comfortable and to appear loving. He tried to play it off like he was just concerned about my well-being, but no, this was very problematic and inappropriate, but at the time, I didn't understand that it was, and I didn't tell anyone. This also qualifies as desensitizing a child, meaning making a child feel less sensitive to what's happening, making the child feel that it's normal.

I remember that at this same church, someone asked me if they could look in the back of my pants to see what size I wore. This one was more subtle, but still suspicious, as my size was pretty obvious. Fortunately, this person didn't get to look in the back of my pants, and I can't even remember exactly why, but I just remember the person reassuring me that was all they would do. Red flag and more desensitizing.

Ever heard of grooming? What exactly is grooming? It is the act of attempting to form a relationship with a child or a young person, with the intention of sexually abusing them. How do you know if someone is grooming you or grooming your child? When I was twelve years old, an older individual befriended me. They had gotten close to me and gave me their number, home and cell phone. They referred to me by two specific nicknames that I remember.

Although there were other kids around, this person's interest in me had been piqued. This person was notorious for constantly lavishing me with expensive, beautiful, top-quality gifts.

Literally, the gifts were great over-the-top stuff that I had always dreamed of. I was highly intrigued—not that I didn't have anything nice at home, but these gifts were different.

I remember I had always wanted a personalized name necklace. I told my mom I desired one of those necklaces, but my mom didn't know where to find one. Then bam, out of the blue, this person surprised me with a drop-dead gorgeous personalized name necklace—each letter in my name fit perfectly. I heard name necklaces had limits on how many letters would fit, but this necklace could perfectly fit all eight letters in my name evenly. The print of the necklace was bold, and the necklace was gold. It had come from a top-quality jeweler and came in a beautiful box. I loved this necklace so much that I wore it only during certain occasions. I didn't wear it to school or bathe in it; It was way too special to ruin in any way.

The lavish gifts didn't stop here, though. I got many other exquisite, expensive jewelry pieces, and for one event, this individual even bought me an outfit. They took me to the mall, but not just any mall. I was used to going to typical Macomb or Eastland Mall, but this person took me to a better mall that was farther out and had more stores. This was so special. The person had me try on a few outfits to see which looked best.

Now, although the person lavished me with great gifts, there was also a lot of control with this person. I remember they told me that since they were paying for the outfit, it meant that they were obligated to pick it. My mom wasn't invited to this mall trip. Red flag: isolation. Predators often isolate their victims so they can have more control.

They appear with seemingly good intentions and will often make such excuses as "I'm just looking out for your best interest," or "I'm concerned about you," You shouldn't do this." It's important to examine a person's intentions very closely. Take note that this person took an interest in me when I was twelve. At that age, things can be a bit awkward for a child. At this age, most children are in middle school, and most of us know that middle school can be rough. This is often a time when children are bullied or teased the most. Children at this age are easily influenced; they are going through puberty, which is also hard. They may not understand these changes and how to cope with them, which in turn makes it easy for a predator to creep in, especially since at this age is often when children long to find acceptance and find out who they are.

They may struggle with loving themselves, hence their vulnerability. As for myself, I was definitely in a vulnerable state, especially since I was a twelve-year-old who was struggling with sickness in my body, which made me feel even more awkward and worthless.

My first year of middle school was especially rough and lonely as I was at a new school. I didn't make any friends for a while. This person knew all of this and was taking advantage of the situation. I remember the person would give me lots of advice, and one time, they had bought me a CD. The song was actually about struggling with confidence. When I heard the song, it startled me. How did this person know about my struggles with my confidence when I never mentioned it directly? They may have seemed well-meaning, but truthfully, they were playing on my weaknesses.

Predators often deceptively make vulnerable victims feel loved and confident. It's all a ploy, and it seems too good to be true; but at the same time, predators also subtly tear their victims down by stripping them of their power, subtly destroying their self-esteem. This individual wasn't that nice to me. I didn't quite understand why they treated me the way they did, but being a child, I never questioned them or said anything about how it made me feel. I believed that since they were an adult, they knew better, and of course, I knew that children weren't supposed to challenge adults. They always negatively commented on my appearance and style, and they constantly critiqued my developing body. Anything I wore this person seemed to disapprove of.

Understand this: Healthy relationships that are truly from God build you up, not tear you down. There's a difference between constructive criticism vs. destructive criticism; constant criticism over every little thing is destructive. I felt like this person's obsession over my appearance wasn't normal at all and it made me feel uncomfortable. Yet I just ignored it. As an adult, I never even paid in-depth attention to a child's appearance, ever. This person wanted me to look a certain way that they approved of. Red flag. Although predators seem to have your best interest at heart, the reality is they don't. I can truly say I don't ever recall this person saying anything nice to me. Only the gifts were nice—that's it.

I remember when I completed middle school, I was showing the person pictures from my eighth-grade dinner dance. The person looked at one picture of a group of the girls in their dresses and said none of them looked like they were following God. This comment baffled me. The girls simply had on junior miss dresses. I remember this person had particularly pointed out one girl in the picture and said that she looked very "mature." Red flag. Again, a child is a child. I feel this person overstepped their boundaries almost immediately. They never exactly asked my mom if buying me stuff was okay.

Predators often study their victims very well. They pay close attention to what their victim likes and needs, and the control is usually just subtle suggestions, like, "Oh, don't wear this. Wear that." Or, "I got you this instead." Or "It'll look good if you wore this." It all seems loving, but please pay attention to the signs. Then during events, if I sat next to this person, it was just them and me as this person always sat farther in the back.

They never sat near my family at all or invited them to sit in the back with us. You don't find these types of people at all—they find you, literally. This person found me and formed our relationship. I never ever asked for this person to buy me anything. They just did it. To be completely honest, although I like nice things, I'm not someone who just needs gifts bought for me, especially constantly.

Truthfully, most of the time, children will naturally warm up to a safe, well-meaning adult on their own terms, without any gifts or special treatment.

Every child that's ever warmed up to me as an adult just did so naturally. They could feel what kind of person I was. My genuine intentions were clear. I never had to use any special methods to get a child to like me. Predators often aim to appear squeaky clean to the parents of the victim; unfortunately, they lure the parents too, to gain their trust, which results in access to the child. This is all thoroughly planned out.

Many times, parents cannot believe the person means any harm because of how manipulative they are. I remember the person had made a comment that was a bit disturbing, they told me that I didn't look my age and that I looked like an adult, specifically, due to my style.

Truthfully, I always looked younger than my age, so I don't know why the person had made this comment. It made me uncomfortable, but of course, I didn't say anything. This was another red flag, though. This individual even once referred to me as a very "special little girl." Red flag. Predators often refer to victims as special and unique. This person took advantage of my family because of our neediness, particularly my mom for having a child with sickness.

My mom, of course, wanted answers and help, and this person knew this. You can't tell everyone what is happening in your family with you, your kids, spouse etc. People will take advantage, prey on those things.

We start going to the venue where this person was when I was about six years old. Mind you, though the person was there early on, they didn't actually take any interest in me until age twelve. This person was probably studying me beforehand to pick up on my weaknesses, insecurities, and needs. Parents, always pray over your kids because people are always watching more than you think or know. Understand this: Just as God can send people into our lives, so can The Devil. Discernment is key!

The Devil often tries to counterfeit God. He will send counterfeit people and things that seem appealing. This individual was supposedly someone who held a specific title. Predators often hold big titles: They may be a coach, a minister, a pastor, a big-name producer, etc. Many times, predators have a strong influence, a good-paying job, a high-end career, a lavish lifestyle, expensive clothing or jewelry that they themselves wear, a lavish car, or house, etc. This can even impress the parents, especially if the parents are lower in status. Understand this: The Devil doesn't have to have horns and a pitch-fork. He can show up as the very thing we want and desire.

The Bible says The Devil portrays himself as an angel of light. We would often talk on the phone; this is a way for a predator to gain more information on the child, and to make the child feel more comfortable and be more vulnerable to open up about their life and their problems. Predators love helpless individuals. At twelve years old besides being sick, I had no job or money, so the person was doing what I could not do for myself. Many times, a predator may give themselves a special role in the child's life, such as the best friend, the godparent, an aunt or uncle, a big sister or big brother, etc.

These are all ways of manipulation and ways to get close without seeming too suspicious. Parents, be leery if a person wants to do more activities with your child than they do with their own children, and if a person wants to spend more time with your child than you. I remember in one phone conversation, the person commented that they knew that I liked my clothes to fit short and tight.

Once again, this made me uncomfortable. As a child, I simply wore what was in style. Once a girl's body starts to develop, her clothes may simply fit a little tighter, and that's simply okay. If a girl grows taller or is in heels, it may make her dress or skirt look a bit shorter, and that's okay.

One gift I remember this person bought me was these three little tank-top shirts. They fitted my body well. I say this was a bit of a red flag because since the tops were fitted tank tops, semi tight, it showed that when the person bought them, they had to have been thinking about my body—my shape and size and how my body would look in them. Even with this person's concern for my sickness. Honestly, some people are sincerely supportive, but for other people, it's just an act. Be leery if a person is overly sympathetic and deals with you only when you're doing bad.

Know this: Some people do good works only to look good to people and to earn righteousness, but God knows a true heart. Understand this: Theres's no-good people everywhere. Just because a person does good things, such as going to church, donating money to the poor, or volunteering at homeless shelters, it doesn't mean they are a good person or have good intentions. Fortunately, this person didn't do anything to me physically, as contact got broken after a while, and my family and I stopped attending the same events as this person.

However, this is just a warning of things to look out for.

Parents, if your child does talk to someone older than them, even if it's their blood relatives, always monitor the conversations. Set limits on how long your child is allowed to talk on the phone, and with gift-giving, have limits on what your child is allowed to receive from someone. Teach your children not to be easily impressed by material things.

Children and teens, even if someone just says things that makes you feel uncomfortable, you're not just crazy or overthinking. Pray for discernment, and also talk to your parents about it. If they're not receptive, talk to someone else who will be receptive, another trusted adult, older siblings, etc. Also, know this: Just because someone is an adult doesn't mean that they know everything; can't be wrong and it's okay to voice how you feel; adults should respect children too. Control is also a form of abuse; if a person wants to control you that's a red flag; it's a unhealthy relationship of any kind.

Parents please be careful with telling your children that they have to obey all adults no questions asked. What if an adult is asking them to do something uncomfortable? Be mindful.

Scripture: 1 Corinthians 15:33

Reference
- I Thought I Could Trust Him: Learn the Signs of Grooming and Manipulation,October 14, 2019.
- National Legal Service, Recognizing the Difference Between Love and Controlling Behavior in Relationships:Warning Signs by NLS Admin, December 2023
- Pierce, Rebekah 15 Warning Signs That Help to Identify a Child Predator. March 2023 11-minute read
- The Pragmatic Parent,Common Tricks a Child Predator Uses: Telling Signs of a Child Predator,By Cori, January 1, 2017, Updated July 8, 2024.Vineyard Swimming, Social Responsibility: Six Stages of Sexual Grooming – signs to watch for, report abuse November 12, 2020.

Part 7

What is Attempted rape? Attempted rape means the goal was to carry out the act of rape, but fortunately, the victim gets away and is untouched. Now understand this even attempted rape is still very serious and should be reported.

I had two attempted rape incidents in high school. The first incident, I was in the ninth grade, and I was in the classroom alone, and this boy came in.

He asked me if I could help him get his brush out of his pocket. I was a bit hesitant, but he forced my hand into his pocket farther and farther. Then instead of feeling a brush, I could feel his penis, and it was erect. I immediately withdrew my hand out of his pocket and got away from him.

The next incident, was in the tenth grade. Again, I was alone in the classroom. It was the end of the day, this boy and I were the last two students in the classroom. He would always flirt with me low-key, so with us being alone, he picked me up, literally, and flipped me up on top of the desk and attempted to try to go up under my skirt. Yikes. I immediately hopped up off that desk and dashed out of that classroom, fortunately.

I never told the school about either of these incidents, though I didn't realize this was attempted rape at the time and didn't realize the seriousness of it.

Reference
- Rape Crisis England and Wales. What is sexual assault?

I have experienced attempted rapes in my adulthood as well. Once, I was walking down the street to me some food, this guy pulled up in a red car and asked me where I was going. I just said to get a bite to eat. He then offered me a ride in his car; he was so persistent. I declined, but he slowly became more aggressive, including asking my name. I ignored him and walked even faster. This man was trying to get me in his car so that he could rape me, even possibly kill me. Him acting kind and helpful was just manipulation. Never get in a stranger's car, ever, no matter how nice and helpful they appear.

Once, I was out at a night-club, and a man offered to buy me a drink, so I let him. I thoroughly saw him order it at the bar. So then after I drank it, I was on the dance floor, and he had his friend hand me another drink. I set this drink down and didn't drink it. Then he invited me to come outside with him. I declined. This man had plans to get me drunk enough so he could have full control over me and rape me, and possibly even have his friend help him—that's why he wanted me outside alone, away from everybody.

Encouragement, Advice, and Reflections

1. Night-life safety

If you go to a club or any late-night event, especially one involving alcoholic beverages, to be safe, never take a drink that you didn't see get made, and never drink your drink once you've set it down and left it unattended, as someone could put something in it while you're not watching. There has always been much debate on whether a woman should go out alone at night. The answer is yes, women should be able to go out alone and enjoy themselves during night hours, but while you're out, keep your cell phone on you at all times and make sure it is fully charged enough for the whole night. If you feel yourself getting too intoxicated, stop drinking. Know your limits. Don't even let friends push you to drink beyond your limits, and do not ever leave with someone that you don't know or didn't come with.

If someone interests you, just take their number instead. There is also nothing wrong with bringing items to the club to keep you safe, such as Pepper spray, Mace, etc, just in case anyone tries to get too crazy with you. This advice applies to men too who go out at night. If something does happen, however, please immediately report it to the staff at the club or event. Don't hesitate—reporting can help ensure safety of others who are out as well. Report even if someone just says something that makes you uncomfortable. You deserve to be able to enjoy yourself peacefully wherever you go!

Scripture: Isaiah 54:17

Part 8

Marital rape is something most people don't believe can happen. Why would a person's spouse sexually abuse them? Well, this definitely happens quite often.

If physical, verbal, mental, emotional, and even financial, abuse can take place in a marriage, then so can sexual abuse. I feel that too often, the church encourages women to stay in abusive marriages.

Women are often told to just pray for their husbands. An abusive marriage of any kind is not God's will.

Women are also often told that as long as their husbands take care of the home, that should be reason enough to stay; but truthfully, it should not be. The church doesn't talk about marital rape.

I've heard many churches talk about how sex once you're married should be pure, amazing. Yes it is the will of God for a married couple to have a good, healthy, comfortable sex life; but there should still be consent and boundaries between spouses. There's never any mention of what qualifies as abuse or going too far. What about marriages where threesomes are done? This definitely isn't okay, but there are many marriages where stuff like that takes place. Even if you're married, you have the right to say no to your spouse if you don't truly want to or if there's something that you're uncomfortable with. Love also means to respect!

Reference

- Fisher, SimchaHow the church can help (or hurt) women in abusive marriagesJune 26, 2018.
- Silva, Sandra and Robyn Russell. What Is Marital Rape?Medically reviewed by Janet Brito, PhD, LCSW, CST-S, PsychCentral, Updated on June 23, 2021.

Part 9

Predators are notorious for being online, which allows a person to falsify their persona—meaning they can pretend to be someone they are not. They can lie about their name, age, work, and more.

Sexual abuse via phone, text, and social media can take form of a person constantly pressuring you to send explicit pictures, even to engage in phone sex, explicit conversations via phone or text if you don't want to do any of that. Even if you do agree to an explicit conversation, but if, you don't want to actually see any explicit pictures, but the person sends them anyway or makes you send them pictures of you this is abusive. If a person sends your pictures to others without your permission, it's a form of abuse. If you are a child online or on a cell phone or tablet/iPad, never send an adult any pictures of yourself. If an adult messages you online via social media or just via phone, please tell your parents or a trusted adult in your life and have them help you report it to the police. Never meet up with a stranger you meet online even if they ask.

With all that being said, is it okay to be online at all? Well, if you're an adult, ultimately, that choice is up to you. But be cautious. If you're a child, it's up to your parents. Parents, if you allow your children to be online or to have an electronic device, please keep them safe as much as possible. Having some limits on the time they can spend online or on their electronic devices may be beneficial, as well as monitoring who is online. Please, if your child does encounter a predatory situation online, don't scold or punish them; instead, explain to them the importance of their safety. Can a person online be trustworthy at all? Well, maybe, some people do meet a trustworthy person online; there are even people who find love online. If you're an adult and you meet someone seemingly trustworthy online, take your time to get to know the person by thoroughly communicating. Pray and ask God if they're safe to let into your life, then go from there.

Reference

- NSVRVC. Online Abuse and Trauma.
- RAINN. 5 Red Flags and 5 Tips to Protect Your Child Online. April 10, 2023.
- RAINN. Tips for Safer Online Dating and Dating App Use.

Part 10

2012 was an amazing year for me: So many good opportunities were coming my way. Me turning twenty later that year was what I was anticipating the most. I remember that day like it was yesterday. I was beyond happy and excited to be coming out of my teens and entering into my twenties and becoming a woman. I had set so many big goals, and I was ready to smash them. I had nothing but high expectations. I remember my twentieth birthday in full detail. I went shopping, I remember me and my oldest sister went to a favorite store of mine, and I saw a cute dress I liked, it was red, black, and white and strapless, but they were all out of my size, though. I tried on a few dresses, and then my mom and I went shopping. I remember I went in this boutique in the mall and bought this cute dress. It was black and gray and form-fitting, and one of the arms was out. I loved it so much, and my mom bought me these fly silver chain earrings and baked me a strawberry shortcake. It didn't turn out perfect as she wanted, but I loved it still. Then that Saturday, my family took me out to eat at one of my favorite restaurants, Golden Corral. I wore my new black dress and these gray heeled boots, and my hair was so full, coily, and bright red. I had the absolute best twentieth birthday ever. I now began to envision what the rest of my twenties would be like. I just knew perfect, little did I know, though, that at the age of twenty would be when I would lose my virginity. I had been a virgin all the way up to this point in my life. I never had sex while I was in high school, never even had a boyfriend, nor had I ever even kissed a guy. I had only hugged a guy before, and it was a very G-rated hug, nothing below the waist.

Now, since I was getting older, it did start to cross my mind. I did begin to think about it a bit more. I was just curious. You hear other people talk about sex so you start wondering what it's like.

When I was growing up, no one really talked to me about sex in detail, or at all, truthfully. Of course, growing up in the church, I just mainly heard how it was bad if you weren't married.

Throughout my childhood, my mom didn't allow me to hear or see sexual content at all—music, TV, or even just conversations about sex. When I would ask her questions about sex, she didn't like it and would scold me a bit, so I just assumed that sex was all bad, which made me stay away from it by all means.

Reference
- Schroeder, Joanna Why You Should Talk About Sex With Your Kids Every. Single. Day.

One particular day, Tuesday, April 2, 2013, is one I'll never forget. I was going to school for fashion design during this time, I vividly remember waking up that morning and getting ready for school.

Now, to be completely honest, I had a feeling that on this day, something was going to happen—something bad. But I pressed on to school, nevertheless. While I was at school, and after I got out of my first class, I was approached by an older guy. He stopped and spoke to me. He was quite talkative, and even a bit flirty.

Now I'd seen him around a few short times before, maybe twice. He consistently walked with me and continued to talk. It was later in the day, like, close to evening when he approached me. He began to get even flirtier and started pressuring me to do sexual things, but of course, I declined. I didn't know him, and we were in public, but he was persistent. I remember exactly what I was wearing: It was a colorful fitted dress that I had gotten from Forever 21. It had colorful leaves all over it, and I had on some black leopard-print tights, and some light-brown cowgirl boots, and I was carrying a bright yellow-and-pink clear rectangle purse, also from Forever 21.

I had my hair braided; they were long, thin box braids that were blonde, black, and pink. I had my braids styled in an updo this day, and I had on some fuchsia-pink lipstick from Revlon. Now as we were walking, this guy put his fingers up my dress a bit. It made me uncomfortable, though, so I kept declining, but he persisted. I remember he told me he had a condom with him and reassured me that he would use it, and he asked me if I was on birth control.

Next, we ended up going into another area, so he got me alone there. It was way in the back upstairs stairwell on the third floor. He pressured me even more and just got right close up on me in my face, pleading for us to take things farther. He then pulled his bare penis out of his pants. It was very erect. Yikes. At this point, it was as though I had no choice but to do what he wanted. He then pulled my dress up, and pulled down the black leopard-print tights and orange panties that I had on. I was so shocked by his aggressive persistence. Then he put his erect penis in me raw, no condom, and he began to thrust hard and fast. I was so confused. I didn't know how to feel. I was very nervous. After the first few thrusts, I asked him to stop, but that just made him keep going, thrusting even harder. He then asked if I wanted him to kiss me. I felt pressured as he was right up in my face, so I just let him. He kissed me twice, quickly, which was also uncomfortable for me, and then he kept thrusting.

I was super tight down there, but he didn't care; he kept on, no slowing down.

He was so rough. I remember he tried to almost lift me to get in me deeper; however, his roughness made me hit my head on the wall, and when I hit my head on the wall, my updo hairstyle came loose, yet he did not care. He didn't stop to say, "Sorry, how do you feel? Did I hurt you? He just continued thrusting, with absolute zero remorse. I tried pushing him off me multiple times, but I couldn't. He was heavy on me, and when I pushed back, he kept pushing himself into me harder and thrusting more and more, non-stop. He wouldn't let up at all.

We first began standing up; then he tried to bend me over and penetrate me that way, but I was extremely uncomfortable with that, so then he got me on the floor and thrust. He ignored my tightness and just thrust ever so hard continuously. I truly didn't know what exactly to say. This went on for hours. I didn't think he would ever stop. "Yikes. It got later and later then finally he did stop.

I remember just walking away afterward feeling so shocked, confused, and numb, like, what just happened? I wasn't expecting that to happen at all, like, was it bad, I pondered? I began to contemplate, did I really want it? Did I enjoy it? So many thoughts ran through my mind afterward. I remember that when he stopped, I immediately ran to the bathroom and asked God, was I wrong? And why did it happen?

Afterward. I called a friend of mine and told her what happened, and she asked me if I knew the guy and if we were dating. I told her no, that I had pretty much just met him. I just had so many thoughts. Then the fact that he was in me raw the whole time, I wondered, what if I were to become pregnant or catch an STD; sexually transmitted disease. "Yikes."

I didn't know what to expect or what was going to happen. I felt a mix of emotions, and oddly enough, I had two dreams prior to this. In one dream, I saw something happening between me and a guy at the school. I didn't see all the details, but I just brushed it off. Then I had a vivid dream about being pregnant, but in the dream, I was single. I knew very vaguely who the father was; it was supposed to be someone that I had gone to school with. In the dream, my family was asking me questions about him, I didn't see fully how he looked, but he was slim, which, even more oddly, this guy who raped me was just that. "Yikes."

All I could think of was what if we really had made a child?

The next few weeks after this encounter, I did start to feel a bit different in my body. I had constant headaches, and my appetite started diminishing; however, I didn't want to talk about it with my family because I didn't know how they would react. I didn't want judgement. How do you really talk to your family about something like that? Truthfully, I never had talked to them about any touchy subjects at all, and I felt fear that if they found out, they would potentially disown me and I would no longer be worthy of their love because I committed what most churches and Christians believed was a big sin. I constantly wondered, *Did I really do it? Or was it done to me?* I thought, *No, this can't be rape.* Because in my mind, I thought that in order for a situation to be rape, the incident had to take place like outside in an empty secluded alley with the victim screaming for help and a weapon involved.

Also, though I was only twenty I believed that adults didn't get raped, only children. In my mind, I just brushed it off and thought, *This is what grown folks do. Grown folks have sex. It's life*. I told myself if I became pregnant, I would just keep the baby and raise it alone. If I had an STD, though, I would need to go to a doctor and get checked out, but that would also be too embarrassing to tell my family. They would then think I was just having unprotected sex carelessly, willy-nilly. Also, being a Christian, I felt this wouldn't be a good look for me because it would make it seem that I was just sinning with no remorse. This was just Satan putting fear and lies into my mind, though. However, I needed to say something. Either way, regardless of what would happen next, it was very hard, extremely hard, and things only got even harder as the weeks went by. The headaches continued to get worse and worse, and I was struggling greatly in school.

I'll never forget that at school, I had a career counselor who I was super close with and talked to all the time. This counselor was a Christian guy. I'll never forget him; he was so encouraging, I talked to him for hours about everything.

Now, I did mention the situation to him. I brought up how I was feeling, so he asked, was I sexually active? I told him some of what happened, but I didn't tell him the exact details of how it happened. He brought up the possibility of me being pregnant, and I thought with him being a Christian and the fact that he was married, I had expected him to judge me, but to my surprise, he didn't. He just encouraged me to take care of myself if that was the case and not to worry, God would help me if I was pregnant. That gave me some peace.

I felt slightly better, especially since I still hadn't talked to my family about it all. I remember I missed my period on April 18, 2013. I remember being at school that day, but we were sent home early due to a power outage. When I got home, I took a nap. I woke up, still no period. I began to contemplate that I would have to tell my parents. I told myself that although this wouldn't be an ideal situation, *I'll keep it, I'll raise it, but it'll be such a shock becoming pregnant from this type of situation.*

However, a few days later, my period did come, but it was shorter and much lighter. I started losing weight due to nausea. It was very difficult for me to keep food down. I had looked up some things online and read that you could be pregnant but still get a light period or even still have your period completely. Yikes. I had even heard people say that you can be pregnant and actually still have your periods. I just didn't know how to feel or what was going on in my life at all at this point.

I did so poorly in my last semester of school. Literally, my GPA got all the way down to a 0.5. Yikes. I was academically dismissed. It was no surprise, though. I had actually even dreamt that I was going to be academically dismissed. I had dreamt it twice, but I felt relieved. That way, I could escape all that had happened there and, hopefully, get some rest, but of course, I still thought about the situation and the guy. I was very embarrassed to say anything to anybody. I didn't even tell my family that I had been academically dismissed. I just told them I had decided to take a break from school for the summer, but that definitely wasn't the case. I was just feeling so alone at this point in my life. I remember that summer, being alone in my bedroom bawling my eyes out, feeling that my life was completely ruined and there was nothing that I could do at all literally. It seemed every good thing for me had now gone down the drain. I started developing these intense feelings toward myself. I started disliking myself a lot, and I continued thinking about the situation, but I kept convincing myself that I enjoyed it.

Over the next few months, I just started feeling all the way different.

However, I wasn't pregnant or had any STDS, thankfully, but I never started feeling exactly like myself again. I began feeling down. I didn't have any passion anymore. I was very lethargic. I remember afterward, I had really bad restless legs at night when I tried to sleep, better known as restless leg syndrome (RLS). I couldn't understand why, my appetite changed more. I began binge-eating on sweets constantly; this made me gain some weight in the following months. I wanted to get rid of the panties I had on that day, literally. I no longer wanted to wear those orange panties. I felt that they were bad every time I looked at them. I thought about what happened while I was wearing them, and that made me feel uncomfortable. I also had some rectal bleeding for a bit. "Yikes." This was also due to all the stress and trauma my body had been through. I just blocked everything out, though I felt I still needed to continue living my life and have a plan for my future. In my mind, I didn't want to be an overgrown loser living at home with no prospects, so I decided to enroll in cosmetology school. This was a coping mechanism for me deep down, a way to escape my horrible reality and to experience something seemingly positive.

Cosmetology school was unknowingly a way of safety for me. It was a way for me to avoid being around men as the school was female dominated. Only one man was there, that was it.

Many times, as people, our bodies put up the flight response after traumatic events, which means an automatic physiological reaction to a perceived threat. The body makes a way to escape to safety.

Reference
- American Academy of Sleep Medicine. Restless Legs Syndrome. Last reviewed 8/2013
- Cleveland Clinic. Restless Legs Syndrome.
- Dalrymple Kristy PhDDoes Stress Cause Weight Gain? Brown Health University June 4, 2024.
- Mayo Clinic Staff Weight Loss: Gain Control of Emotional Eating:Find Out How Emotional Eating Can

Sabotage Your Weight Loss Efforts and Get Tips to Get Control of Your Eating Habits.
- RAINN, Effects of Sexual Violence.
- Taylor, Martin What Does Fight, Flight, Freeze, Fawn Mean? Medically reviewed by Smitha Bhandari, MD WebMD June 24, 2024.

Encouragement, Advice, and Reflections

1. Homosexuality after rape
2. Sexual pleasure during rape
3. STDs from rape
4. Rape on college campuses

For some people being raped changes their sexuality completely, resulting in homosexuality. I've seen many individuals become gay after being raped. If this is you, I promise you that God is going to restore your sexuality to what He intended it to be. I break off Satan's confusion over your life!

What about if the sex was pleasurable? Does that still mean it was rape? Yes, even if the sex was pleasurable and you had an orgasm. When raped, the body can still react as if it was consensual sex, but this doesn't discount the act as rape. Remember, as mentioned all throughout this chapter, manipulation is often a tool used in rape, so don't be fooled by how pleasurable it seemed. Not all rape is violent! Think of this: If a person smacks you, it may not be painful, but does that mean that they didn't really smack you? Take heed.

If you unfortunately do catch an STD from being raped, it is not your fault. Have no shame, and seek treatment as soon as possible. No matter what the extent of the STD, God will heal you. Amen!

Unfortunately, college students have higher risks of sexual abuse. As mentioned earlier in this chapter, that school is a place that predators commonly inhabit. All schools should have better safety measures. In Fact, the School system should talk more about this issue. Now, ultimately, the school where my rape had occurred ended up getting permanently shut down, literally. This was later in that year. Truthfully, it was for the best for the school to close. That way, my rapist couldn't do any more harm to the other young women there.

Reference
- RAINN. Receiving Medical Attention.
- RAINN. Campus Sexual Violence: Statistics.
- Wolters, Lauren and Macy Smith Sexual Violence Against Female College Students in the United States, *Ballard Brief* Spring 2020.

After my rape, I knew that I wasn't gay. However, I still had many conflicting feelings.

I wanted to learn more about sex, and to do so, I began dabbling in pornography so that I could get more clarity on sex and what it was supposed to be like," I thought this could help me.

I also began to try to have relationships with dudes, but the relationships that I encountered just turned out to be continued rapes; however, I was still in denial; I continued thinking it was all normal, just like my first rape, and ultimately, I just wanted to be loved and accepted by all means, which made me willing to tolerate anything—literally whatever seemed good. The Devil wanted to completely distort my view of sex. Pornography is also a form of sexual abuse in many ways. Know this: Filming a person could lead to later exploitation, and then anyone can see it, which could then damage someone's character. Also, in pornography, there's often no consent to the acts being done.

Reference
- Mohammed, Farahnaz.The Repetition Compulsion: Why Rape Victims Are More Likely to Be Assaulted Again, Girl's Globe,August 4, 2015.
- P. Javier Pornography and It's Impact on Sexual Exploitation, SOS international February 16, 2023.

One of my rapes happened on the job, yet again, I kept silent and didn't realize how serious it was. This person even tried to get me fired by saying some things, not in regard to the rape, but some other trivial things. For those of you reading my book who work, I pray for your safety in your job. You deserve to be able to work peacefully.

Reference
- Altus, Gavin.What is Sexual Abuse In the Workplace? "Sentient, February 16, 2024."

In early 2022 I kept thinking back to 2013. Everything about that year was heavy on my mind. I had uncomfortable feelings that I couldn't erase. Please know this: With sweeping trauma under the rug, pretending that it didn't happen, eventually, the feelings of the incident will come back up no matter how long ago it was. Trauma doesn't automatically go away. It must be thoroughly dealt with. I remember I was alone in my bedroom, and I thought about what happened on April 2, 2013. I said to myself, *That was really problematic, It should not have happened. That was rape.* I had finally realized what truly happened to me. However, it was still difficult to tell anyone.

My mom had actually gotten a revelation about my rape before I had even told her. In early 2021, her, myself and my dad had went to my auntie's church. After the service, the pastor approached her and said to her, Your daughter is healing from abuse. This statement caught my mom off guard, but she knew there was something to this statement. However, one night in 2022, a few weeks after I realized what happened to me, my mom and I were on the telephone talking, and that's when I was able to finally tell her. And then she brought up what the pastor said the year before. My mom was angry about the situation; she wanted revenge, but I calmed her down and reminded her that God was fighting for me. I had eventually realized my other rapes as well. For years, I blamed myself and just deemed myself promiscuous, not realizing that I had been forced, pressured, and manipulated all of those times. The Devil wanted to keep me in bondage to sexual abuse and in bondage to unforgiveness toward myself. My God brought me out. Amen!

Encouragement, Advice, and Reflections

1. Non supportive parents
2. How to support others who were raped

The unfortunate reality is that many parents will not believe their child if they tell them that they were raped, and they won't do anything about it, especially if the rape was committed by a family member or close family friend, but rest assured and know this The Bible says that when your mother and father forsake you that The Lord will take care of you. Amen!

Scriptures:Psalm 27:10; Isaiah 49:15

Jesus is a mother, father, friend, lover, mentor, and so much more! He is Emanuel (God with us). The Wonderful Counselor. We are never alone. Amen!

Scriptures: Matthew 1:23; Isaiah 9:6

Some people are just not mentally and emotionally mature enough to be able to understand certain touchy topics, such as this. If you don't have support from your family through this, don't even take it personal. God will send you the right support that you need.

If someone expresses to you that they were raped, here's what you can do:Listen, embrace them, show them love, and make them feel it genuinely, encourage them to speak up when they feel ready, check on them consistently, be their shoulder to cry on when needed, encourage them to seek out professional help, pray with and for them, and, if they're not a believer, point them to God.

Reference
- Rape Crisis Scotland Supporting someone who has experienced sexual violence: Information for Parents.

CHAPTER TWELVE
I LOVE LIFE

I continued feeling better about my life overall, and I had continued going to therapy. I had soon found a new therapist. Now, she had told me that she was also a minister and had a group I could join. The group was online, so I joined it. I ended up liking the group; it boosted my faith in many ways. Then she had told me about a few other groups that I could join. I joined another group that I ended up loving. I felt supported instead of judged in these groups, which was important to me. In my two groups, it was all women, young and old, but they were all so nice, loving, caring, and welcoming. No drama at all! I decided to continue to boost my faith and learn more about God. In one of the groups, we talked about book writing and telling your story for God's glory. This had really inspired me, and this was God getting me into my true purpose.

During this time, I kept having these recurring dreams about myself. In these dreams, I was younger, a child up through age twenty five, which were the ages that The Devil attacked me in the most. Now, at first, I didn't quite understand these dreams, but soon I realized that God was restoring the years I lost back to me. In these dreams, I was always dressed in the color yellow, which biblically represents honor and covenant. God was giving me honor for all my shame and restoring my covenant. Amen! In one dream, I had this extreme state of joy that I had never experienced. Now, at first, I thought this dream was God calling me home early, but no! I didn't have to die in order to receive my joy. God gave me Heaven on earth. He will do the same for you. Amen!

Scriptures: 1 Peter 5:10; Jeremiah 30:17

Understand that restoration is a process; it's not overnight, but in due time, you will be restored. Will The Devil still attack you while you're being restored? Most definitely. Because The Devil couldn't take me out with all that he tried in the past, he sent one of his demons to take me out literally.

In May of 2023, God allowed me to see in the realm of the spirit. I was all alone in my bedroom, and I looked over to my left and saw a black demon with a deviant grin on the side of my bed, sitting in the chair on the side of my bed. Yikes.

However, I wasn't scared, though. Being in The Spirit I immediately went to praying loud and bold, nonstop. I knew for sure the goal of this demon was death, but I had no fear. I continued praying. So next, this demon had the audacity to try to argue with me. He began trying to tear me down and tell me who I wasn't and what I didn't have, yet I continued in prayer and then I snapped back at him, and I yelled with confidence, "I don't care what you think about me—I know God loves me—I am fearfully and wonderfully made."

The demon then grew silent, threw his hands up, and left. Amen! Satan and his demons have no authority over my restoration. Jesus purchased it for me on the cross. Amen! Satan was just mad about all that I was doing for the kingdom of God and desired to stop it. But no!

In the Summer of 2023, I joined yet another group. This group was mixed, with men and women, but one lady in this group had invited me to the church that was a part of these groups. She invited me to come to a Tuesday-morning Bible study. At this time in my life, I was only viewing church online, but I figured, why not give this church a try. After all, it was right up the street from me anyway. I went, and I loved it. I continued in my groups and went back the next Tuesday, and my mom accompanied me. She loved it as well.

Now a few weeks had passed, and I felt led to join the church. I told my mom, and she was happy and encouraged me to do so. I alerted everyone in my groups, and they were all so excited. I ended up joining in September, a few weeks before my birthday, and it was the absolute best birthday present for me. I met so many amazing people at the church who loved me and supported me, including my co-author, Ms. Lorian Tompkins. When we met, we just clicked instantly, and I told her about this book God told me to write, and she instantly supported me. God puts you where you need to be for a purpose. My church family is my "true family." Family isn't about blood it's about those who love you for you and who support you no matter what, those who have your best interest.

Shortly after I joined the church, my parents and siblings followed. They loved it as well! I know without a doubt that I belong at my church. God has confirmed it to me numerous times. I feel like out of every church I'd ever been to in my entire life, this one was the absolute right fit. I've even had more encounters with God at this church. Amen! Hallelujah! My church is true to its name: "Love Life Family Christian Center," At this church, I can attest that I have felt nothing but pure, real love. This wasn't the case at some of the other churches that I attended, but here, it's definitely a representation of God's love and a representation of what family truly is. My church family keeps me fed, both spiritually and physically. I'm just way too blessed. Amen! Hallelujah!

Scriptures: 1 John 3:18; 1 Corinthians 13: 4–8; Matthew 9:16—-17; Habakkuk 2:2— 3; Jeremiah 30:2; Ephesians 4:11—16; John 13:35

END-OF-BOOK POEM

Young and for G.O.D sprung! Good news Jesus brung! Through my struggles like a wet towel I hung! Though my struggles out of the dirt I sprung! Trouble with my lungs, but God healed me a ton, and He still ain't done! Miss Miracle in 1994, beads diaper and cereal! To God My Father, hello! My life smooth like Jell-O! The Holy Spirit keeps me warm like cocoa. My story now you know!

73 FUN FACTS

ABOUT SHALONDA

1. At age three, Shalonda's older sister confidently spoke to Tracy to tell her that she was going to have another child and that the child would be a girl. At such a young age, she had prophesied her little sister's birth.
2. Shalonda was originally going to be named Tiffany or Jessica by her mom, Tracy, but her dad picked the name *Shalonda*, and everyone loved it.
3. God revealed to Shalonda that He knew she was going to follow him. He revealed to her that He knows who will follow Him from the time that they are created.
4. God revealed to Shalonda that He allowed her close relationship with her mom to happen for a purpose.
5. Writing was always Shalonda's passion. As a child, she kept a notebook and a pen with her. She would write many things, such as songs, movie and sitcom ideas, etc, and in school, she always excelled in English. In January 2025, God revealed to Shalonda that writing was her true calling.
6. Shalonda's favorite color has always been red. Biblically, the color red represents the blood of Jesus; it also represents victory.

7. Shalonda donated to St. Jude Children's Hospital for a few years due to her love and passion for helping others.
8. Shalonda's mom prayed over and anointed every house the family ever lived in with oil; she anointed every area of each home, every room, every single part, as well as the inside and outside.
9. Shalonda was in a fashion show when she was nineteen. She modeled her own outfit that she had made!
10. Shalonda loves flavored coffee, especially iced coffee. And don't forget doughnuts! Yum.
11. Shalonda loves candles.
12. Shalonda's favorite genres of music are jazz, rock 'n' roll, neo-soul, '70s and '80s music!
13. Due to her closeness with her mom, Shalonda has her mom's name tattooed on her. She got it done one Mother's Day and surprised her mom!
14. Shalonda and her mom loved the movie *Look Who's Talking*!
15. Shalonda and her mom loved *The Brady bunch* and Shalonda would beg her mom to give her curly pigtails like *Cindy Brady*!
16. Both of Shalonda's sisters' names begin with an *S* as well. Her little sister's name is the most similar to hers—it's ShaRonda.
17. Shalonda loves stuffed animals.
18. Shalonda's middle name is Shatese, and many people actually call her by that name instead!
19. Shalonda also enjoys acting and theater. She's been in plays at church and in school.
20. Originally, Shalonda planned on going to college and majoring in fashion design and minoring in forensic science!

21. Fall is Shalonda's favorite season. Bring on the pumpkin spice!
22. Shalonda spoils her mom, especially with clothes from Venus!
23. Shalonda is good at making cheesecake!
24. Shalonda loves seafood.
25. Shalonda hates macaroni and cheese.
26. Shalonda's favorite ice creams are mint chocolate chip, rainbow sorbet, and Superman!
27. Shalonda's favorite scripture is Psalm 139:14, which she also has tattooed on her!
28. Shalonda loves long, warm baths.
29. Shalonda's favorite wine is White Zinfandel.
30. Shalonda's favorite restaurant is Cooper's Hawk.
31. When she was a child, Shalonda's family always went to the restaurant old country buffet, which no longer exists.
32. Shalonda's family loved Kmart.
33. Shalonda used to collect butterflies.
34. Shalonda is an introvert.
35. Shalonda loves Looney Tunes.
36. Shalonda likes to paint.
37. Shalonda got her first tattoo at twenty one. It's on her wrist, and it says "pretty girl."
38. Shalonda loves abstract art.
39. Shalonda doesn't like mistreatment of children or animals.
40. Shalonda had a Hello Kitty—themed bedroom and telephone when she was twelve! She loves cats but is allergic to them unfortunately.
41. Shalonda loves '70s and '80s fashion, hair, and makeup.
42. Shalonda's parents met at her maternal grandmother's store

43. Shalonda has a desire to visit outer space one day.
44. Although Shalonda and her mom are very close, they are different as night and day.
45. Shalonda desires to learn how to play the guitar.
46. Shalonda used to collect sea-shells.
47. Shalonda desires to ride a hot air balloon one day.
48. Shalonda loves lemon water.
49. Shalonda loves taking pictures.
50. Shalonda's favorite type of cake is red velvet.
51. Although Shalonda's birthday is way at the end of September, she celebrates the entire month!
52. Shalonda loves cotton candy.
53. Both of Shalonda's sisters were born via C-section. Shalonda was the only one born vaginally.
54. When Shalonda's mom gave birth to her she didn't have to push or anything—-Shalonda just eased out, her mom looked down as she was in the hospital bed and saw Shalonda's head halfway out!
55. Shalonda's family loved going to Kings Island and Cedar Point. They made it a tradition to go every summer.
56. Shalonda used to dislike her name when she was younger and wanted it to be Tanesha or Angelina!
57. Although she didn't pursue it as a professional career, Shalonda enjoys sewing and making clothes, and even jewelry, when she gets in the mood.
58. Shalonda sold her handmade jewelry in high school
59. Shalonda loves Valentine's Day candy.
60. Shalonda went trick-or-treating only once in her lifetime, when she was seven, and she found it very boring.
61. Shalonda never ever believed in Santa Claus, the tooth fairy, or the Easter bunny!

62. Shalonda isn't a morning person, but as she's gotten older, she has adjusted.
63. Shalonda never liked the dark. She didn't start sleeping with her bedroom light off till age twenty-eight literally.
64. Shalonda can't dance, but her mom can.
65. Growing up, Shalonda's favorite singer was Brandy. She had all her dolls and posters. She even had a baby doll that she named after her.
66. Shalonda loved the Spice Girls and had their dolls and posters as well and the movie on VHS.
67. Shalonda had a pet rabbit before; his name was Oliver.
68. Shalonda loves Amazon.
69. As a child, Shalonda once gave her mom a big birthday party.
70. Shalonda had her first crush at three years old. He was an older boy on her block.
71. When Shalonda was ten, she had written a petition to get *Muppet Babies* put back on the air.
72. Shalonda's favorite animal is koalas. She had a pet dog who she affectionately called the "Fuzzy Koala."
73. The day Shalonda got saved, she had actually just gotten out of the hospital due to an asthma attack, yet The Devil couldn't stop her! Amen!
74. Bonus fun fact: God told Shalonda that her book would be completed on Easter (Resurrection Sunday), and that was so! It's amazing because Easter is all about Jesus's work and it's completion, and it's Shalonda's favorite holiday besides New Year's. As a child, Shalonda always enjoyed doing speeches at church for Resurrection Sunday.

NEW PICTURES

"Rip to my fuzzy koala! Mommy loves you forever, your legacy lives on."

MEET MY CO- AUTHOR

Lorian Janine Tompkins is a special education teacher, singer-songwriter, starting entrepreneur, and author originally from Detroit, Michigan. She now lives in Clinton Township, Michigan, establishing her career as an artist and storyteller. Lorian hopes that through storytelling in both writing and music, those who have felt silenced can be empowered to use their voices.

www.ingramcontent.com/pod-product-compliance
Lightning Source LLC
Chambersburg PA
CBHW040303170426
43194CB00021B/2881